CHORDS & PROGRESSIONS FOR
JAZZ
& POPULAR KEYBOARD

KENNETH BAKER

AMSCO PUBLICATIONS
NEW YORK/LONDON/SYDNEY

Order No. AM 31584
US International Standard Book Number: 0.8256.2286.7
UK International Standard Book Number: 0.7119.0014.7

Exclusive Distributors:
Music Sales Corporation
257 Park Avenue South, New York, NY 10010 USA
Music Sales Limited
8/9 Frith Street, London W1V 5TZ England
Music Sales Pty. Limited
120 Rothschild Street, Rosebery, Sydney, NSW 2018, Australia

Printed in the United States of America by
Vicks Lithograph and Printing Corporation

CONTENTS

PREFACE

This book is intended mainly for the "amateur" keyboard player who would like to explore the fascinating world of modern Jazz Harmony, but has little or no background in Musical Theory.

The HALF STEP (SEMITONE) rather than the SCALE has been favored as the basic working unit, since the concept of "half step" is immediately accessible to the novice, whereas the precise details of 12 Major Scales are not.

Chord "types" have been reduced to just four. All other Chord Types (as described in other books) are constructed here by the use of simple "Added Notes" expressed in terms of "half steps" rather than "Intervals" (the "traditional" approach).

The "UPR" – Usual Playing Range – (SECTION TWO, p. 8) must be considered only a general guide to keyboard chord voicing: a useful teaching "aid", no more, no less. If the student on occasion wishes to play higher or lower than recommended, that is entirely up to him, providing of course that the results are musical.

Finally, it is important that the student should work conscientiously through the Exercises given at the end of each SECTION. This can be a most revealing way to test one's understanding of what has gone before.

NOTE: In this book "+" and "–" signs (meaning sharpen (sharp) and flatten (flat) respectively, by one half step) apply only to the numbers which FOLLOW the sign.

e.g.:–

C+5 (C+* for short)	=	C (Major) with a sharpened (sharped) 5th
C–5	=	C (Major) with a flattened (flatted) 5th
C7+9 (C+9 for short)	=	C7 with a sharpened (sharped) 9th
C7.9+11 (C+11 for short) =		C9 with a sharpened (sharped) 11th

(and so on)

*Since this chord is so common the number "5" is often omitted.

Kenneth Baker

SECTION ONE   **CHORD FORMATION**

Basically there are four TYPES of chord used in popular Western music:—

MAJOR
MINOR
DIMINISHED
AUGMENTED

They can be expressed by the following simple formulae:—

MAJOR	4–3
MINOR	3–4
DIMINISHED	3–3
AUGMENTED	4–4

The figures above refer to HALF STEPS (SEMITONES).

HALF STEP OR SEMITONE: The smallest possible distance between notes (white or black) on a modern piano or organ keyboard:

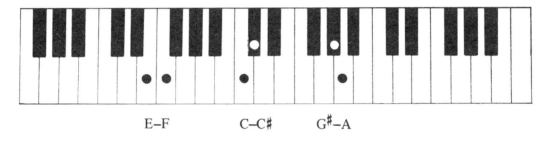

E–F   C–C♯   G♯–A

Three examples of HALF STEPS

As a practical example of how to form a chord let us now construct a chord of C MAJOR:—

C MAJOR = C–4–3

Starting from the note "C" (The letter name of the chord we wish to find), count UP (i.e. to the RIGHT) in HALF STEPS:—

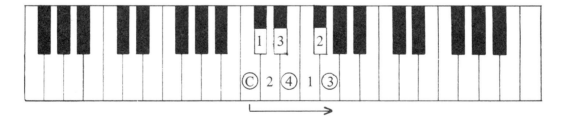

The three notes arrived at:—

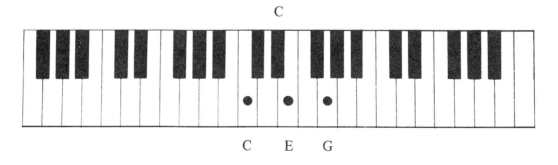

C   E   G

This is the chord of C MAJOR ("C" for short).

Example 2.   AIM:— To construct a chord of B♭ MAJOR (B♭ for short):—

$$B♭ = B♭-4-3$$

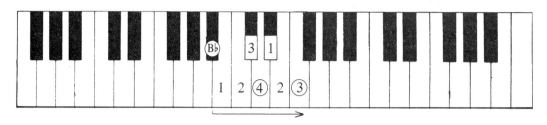

The chord arrived at:—

Bb

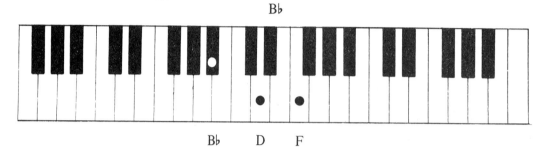

B♭   D   F

Example 3.   AIM:— To construct a chord of C MINOR (Cm for short):—

$$Cm = C-3-4 \text{ (“Minor” formula)}$$

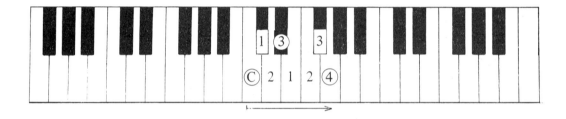

The chord arrived at:—

Cm

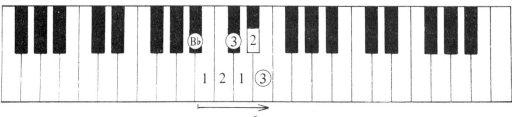

C   E♭   G

Example 4.   AIM:— To construct a chord of B♭ DIMINISHED (B♭dim, or B♭^{O} for short):—

$$B♭^O = B♭-3-3 \text{ (“Diminished” formula)}$$

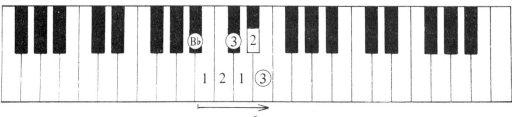

The chord arrived at:−

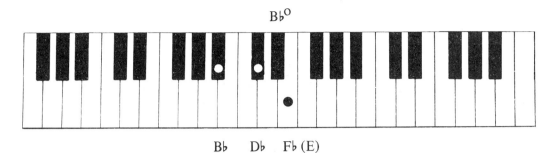

B♭°

B♭   D♭   F♭ (E)

Example 5.   AIM:− To construct a chord of C AUGMENTED (C^{aug}, or C$^+$ for short):−

C$^+$ = C–4–4 ("Augmented" formula)

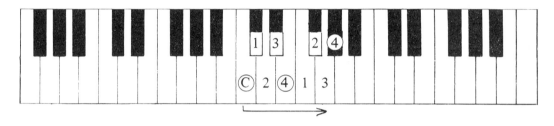

The chord arrived at:−

C$^+$

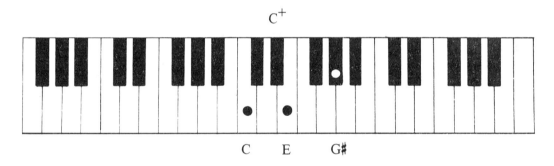

C   E   G♯

Exercise 1.   Find:−

a) B♭ Minor (B♭m)   B♭ D♭ F   g) D Major (D)   D F♯ A ✓
b) C Diminished (C°) C E♭ G♭   h) F Major (F)   F A C ✓
c) B♭ Augmented (B♭$^+$) B♭ D G♭ i) F Minor (Fm) F A♭ C ✓
d) G Major (G) G B D   j) G Diminished (G°) G B♭ D♭ ✓
e) G Minor (Gm) B♭   k) G Augmented (G$^+$) G B E♭ ✓
f) F Diminished (F°) F A♭ B ✓ l) F Augmented (F$^+$) F A D♭ ✓

(Answers on page 95)

SECTION TWO   **INVERSIONS (1)**

Best area for Left Hand chords:—

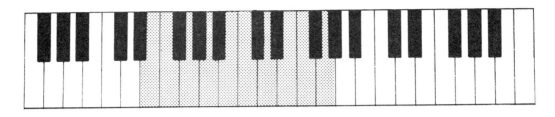

↑
MIDDLE C (organ lower keyboard)

Usual Playing Range (UPR):—

UPR

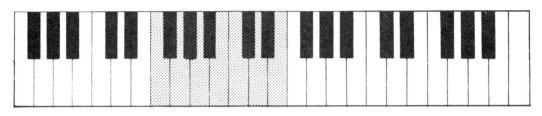

↑
MIDDLE C (organ lower keyboard)

The four "C" chords from SECTION ONE:—

    C Major (C)
    C Minor (Cm)
    C Diminished (C^{O})
    C Augmented (C^{+})

with their notes rearranged to fall into the UPR:—

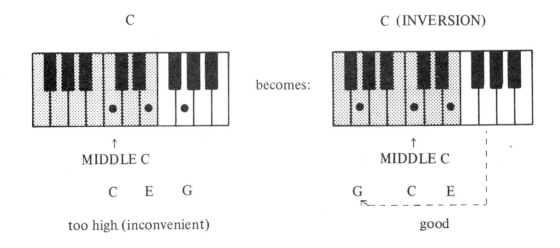

        C   C (INVERSION)

becomes:

↑
MIDDLE C   MIDDLE C

C   E   G   G   C   E

too high (inconvenient)   good

8

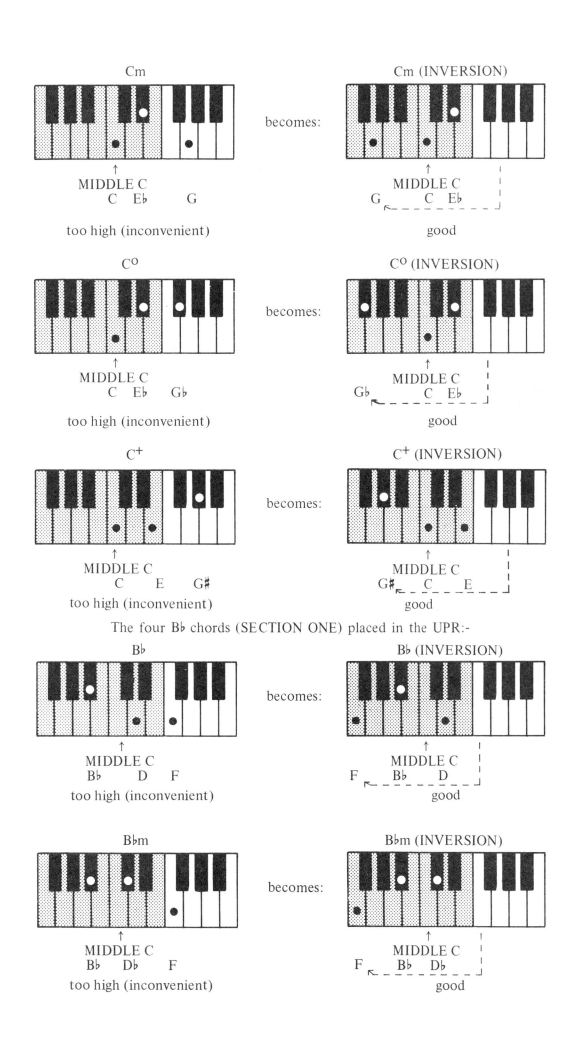

The four Bb chords (SECTION ONE) placed in the UPR:-

9

D 3-3   A 4-4
keep root only ↑1
semitone 3rd note

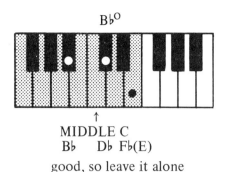

B♭°

MIDDLE C
B♭   D♭   F♭(E)

good, so leave it alone

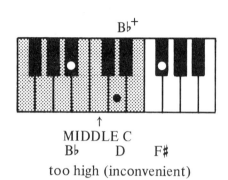

B♭⁺

MIDDLE C
B♭   D   F♯

too high (inconvenient)

becomes:

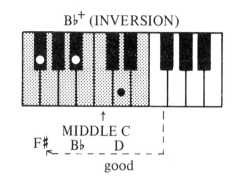

B♭⁺ (INVERSION)

MIDDLE C
F♯   B♭   D

good

Exercise 2.   Find the following chords, altering the order of the notes if necessary to suit the UPR:—

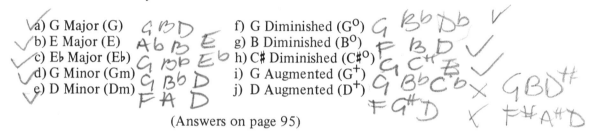

a) G Major (G)   G B D
b) E Major (E)   A♭ B E
c) E♭ Major (E♭)   G B♭ E♭
d) G Minor (Gm)   G B♭ D
e) D Minor (Dm)   F A D

f) G Diminished (G°)   G B♭ D♭ ✓
g) B Diminished (B°)   F B D ✓
h) C♯ Diminished (C♯°)   G C♯ E ✓
i) G Augmented (G⁺)   G B♭ C♭ ✗   G B D♯
                           F G♯ D ✗   F♯ A♯ D
j) D Augmented (D⁺)

(Answers on page 95)

10

SECTION THREE   **ADDED NOTES (1)**

The main note of any chord is called the "ROOT"

C   ⎫   B♭   ⎫
Cm   ⎬   Root = C   B♭m   ⎬   Root = B♭
C⁰   ⎪   B♭⁰   ⎪
C⁺   ⎭   B♭⁺   ⎭

The above are all basic three-note chords.

A note may be added to any basic "three-note" chord, making it into a "four-note" chord.

Three useful "Added Notes" are:—

maj 7
7
6

On the keyboard these three Added Notes lie directly to the LEFT of the Root:—

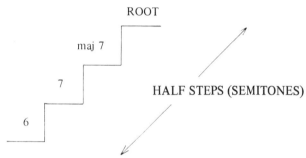

Example 1.   If the Root were "C" the Added Notes would be as follows:—

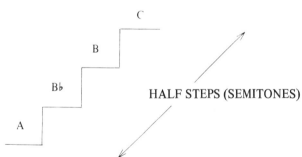

On the keyboard:—

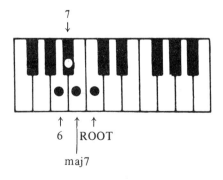

Applying each of the above "Added Notes" to the chord of C:—

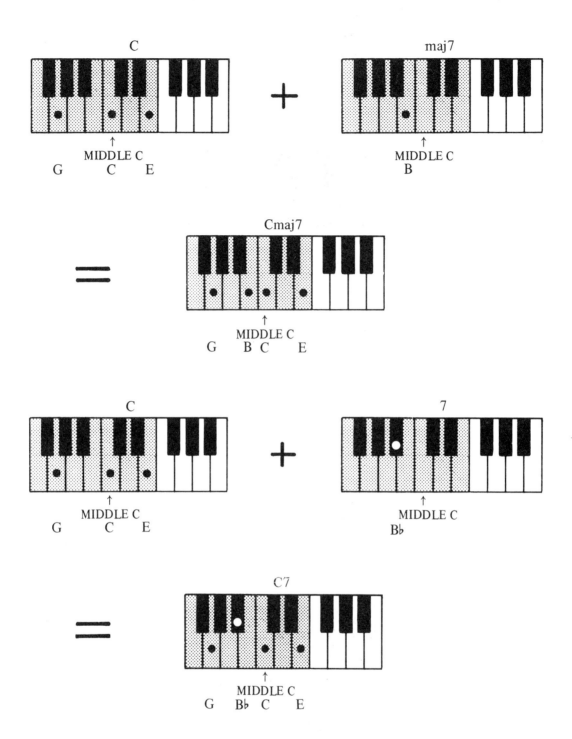

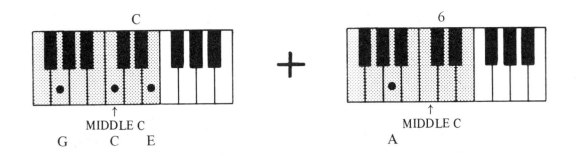

$$C \quad + \quad 6$$

G   C   E   A

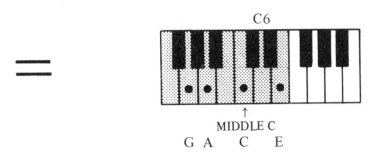

C6

G A   C   E

Example 2.   If the Root were "B♭" the "Added Notes" would be as follows:—

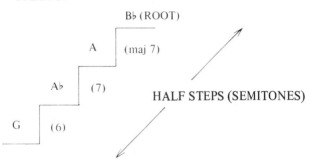

B♭ (ROOT)

A   (maj 7)

A♭   (7)   HALF STEPS (SEMITONES)

G   (6)

On the keyboard:—

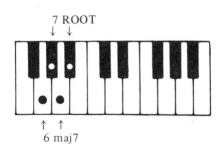

7 ROOT

6 maj7

13

Applying each of the above "Added Notes" to the chord of B♭:—

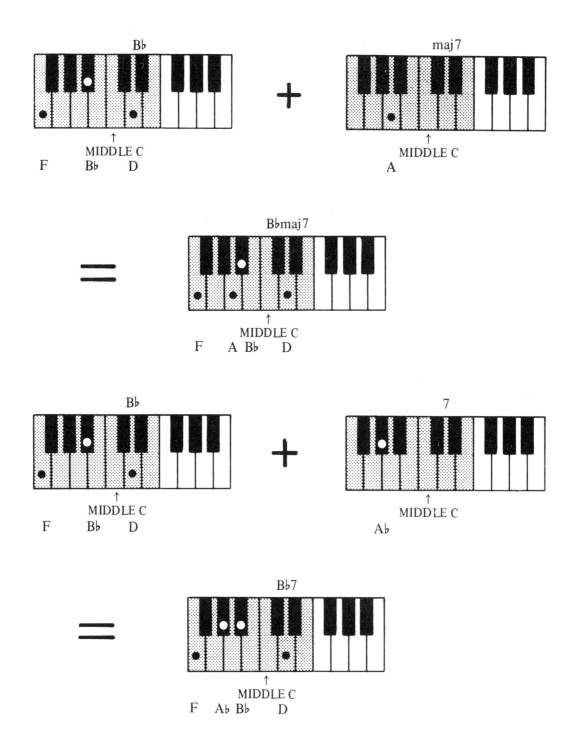

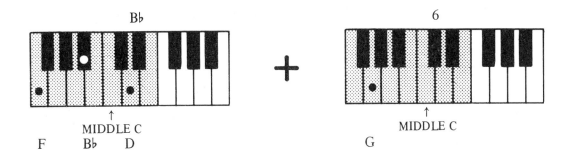

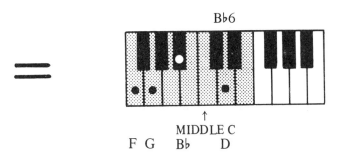

Exercise 3.   Find the following basic Major Chords (three notes each). Check that your chords lie in the UPR (Usual Playing Range):—

a) G   *G B D* ✓
b) D   *F# A D* ✓
c) F   *F A C* ✓
d) E   *G A E*   *G# B E*
e) A   *A C# E* ✓

Exercise 4.   Using the chords of Exercise 3 as a starting point, add notes to obtain the following "four-note" chords (check your UPR in each case):—

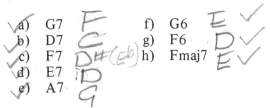

✓ a) G7   *F*   f) G6   *E* ✓
✓ b) D7   *C*   g) F6   *D* ✓
✓ c) F7   *D#(Eb)*   h) Fmaj7 *E* ✓
✓ d) E7   *D*
✓ e) A7   *G*

Exercise 5.   Find the following basic Minor Chords (three notes each). Check your UPR in each case:—

✓ a) Cm   *G C D#/Eb*   d) Fm *F G# C Ab* ✓
✓ b) Gm   *G Bb D*   e) Em *G B E* ✓
✓ c) Dm   *F A D*   f) Am *A C E* ✓

Exercise 6.   Using the chords of Exercise 5 as a starting point, add notes to obtain the following "four-note" chords (check your UPR in each case):—

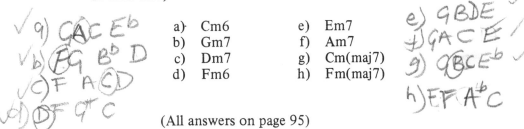

✓ a) *G A C Eb*   a) Cm6   e) Em7
✓ b) *F G Bb D*   b) Gm7   f) Am7
✓ c) *F A C D*   c) Dm7   g) Cm(maj7)
✓ d) *D F G# C*   d) Fm6   h) Fm(maj7)

e) *G B D E* ✓
f) *G A C E* ✓
g) *G B C Eb* ✓
h) *E F A# C*

(All answers on page 95)

SECTION FOUR   CHORD PROGRESSIONS (1)

Progression 1:—   C6 — G7 — C6

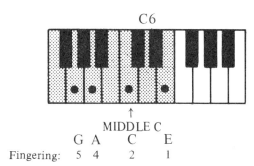

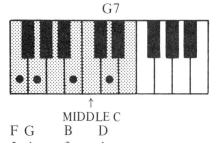

C6
MIDDLE C
G A   C   E
Fingering: 5 4   2   1

G7
MIDDLE C
F G   B   D
Fingering: 5 4   2   1

Organ pedals play "Roots" (i.e. with C6 play Pedal C, with G7 play Pedal G)

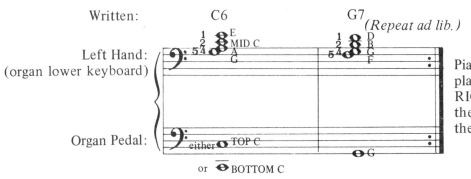

Pianists should also practise playing these chords with the RIGHT HAND whilst playing the low organ pedal notes with the left hand.

Progression 2:—   C6 — F6 — C6

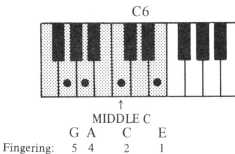

C6
MIDDLE C
G A   C   E
Fingering: 5 4   2   1

F6
MIDDLE C
F   A   C D
Fingering: 5   4   2 1

Written: C6   F6
                            (Repeat ad lib.)

Left Hand:
(organ lower keyboard)

(Pianists play these chords with either hand.)

Organ Pedal:

(Optional left hand for piano.)

TOP C
BOTTOM C
F

16

Progression 2 when played on the organ sounds better if the middle two notes (Middle C and A) are held throughout. Written:—

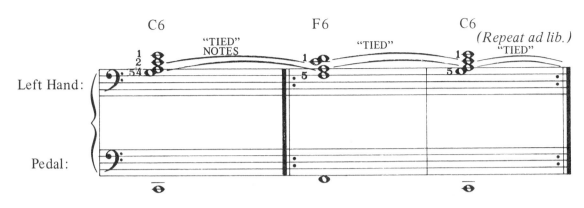

Progression 3:—   C6 — F6 — G7 — C6

Written:

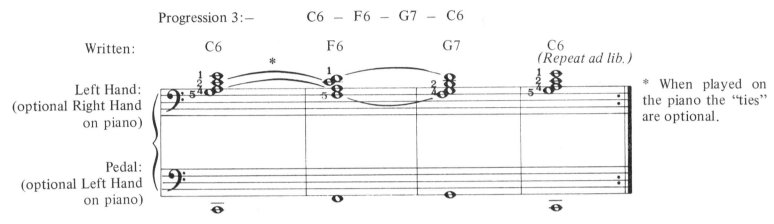

* When played on the piano the "ties" are optional.

Progression 4:—   C6 — Am7 — Dm7 — G7 — C6

Am7 = C6 }
Dm7 = F6 } except for the organ Pedal Note

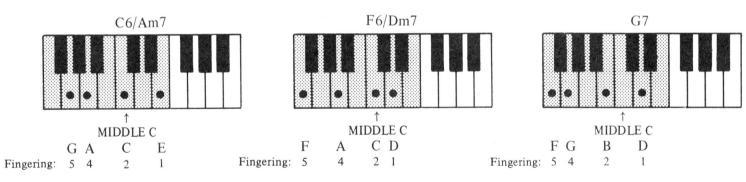

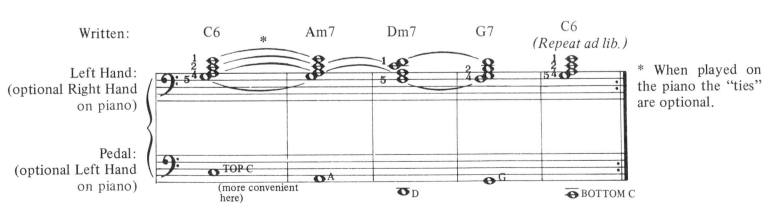

* When played on the piano the "ties" are optional.

Exercise 7.   Revise D7, A7, Cmaj7, Fmaj7 (4 notes each). Check your UPR in each case.

Now play the following Chord Progressions (on organ include pedals; on piano play chords with either hand):—

a) D7   — G7   — D7
b) A7   — D7   — A7
c) C6   — A7   — D7   — G7   — C6
d) Cmaj7 — C6   — F6   — G7   — C6
e) Cmaj7 — Am7   — Dm7   — G7   — C6
f) Cmaj7 — Fmaj7 — Cmaj7
g) Cmaj7 — Fmaj7 — Dm7   — G7   — C6

(Answers on pages 95 and 96)

SECTION FIVE INVERSIONS (2)

Some four-note chords have a useful Inversion or Position which lies slightly out of the UPR (Usual Playing Range) one way or the other:—

G7 (Normal Position)

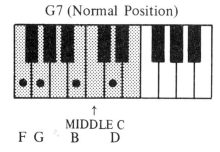

MIDDLE C

F G   B   D

G7 (High Position)

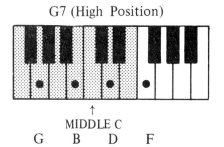

MIDDLE C

G   B   D   F

both useful

Gmaj7 (Normal Position)

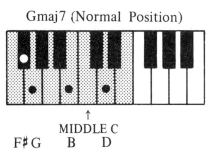

MIDDLE C

F♯ G   B   D

discordant

Gmaj7 (High Position)

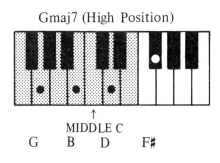

MIDDLE C

G   B   D   F♯

less discordant

E7 (Normal Position)

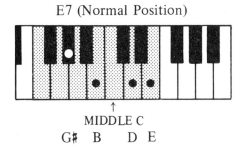

MIDDLE C

G♯ B   D E

E7 (Low Position)

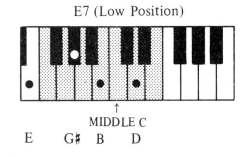

MIDDLE C

E   G♯ B   D

both useful

Exercise 8.   Find: a) Gm7 (High Position)
b) Gm(maj7) (High Position)
c) Emaj7 (Low Position)
d) E♭maj7 (Low Position)

(Answers on page 96)

19

SECTION SIX   **ADDED NOTES (2)**

Applying the "maj 7", "7", and "6" to DIMINISHED and AUGMENTED chords:—

DIMINISHED   AUGMENTED

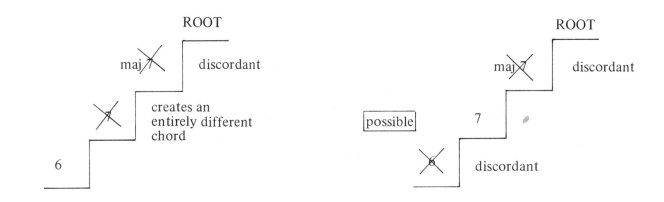

Examples:—

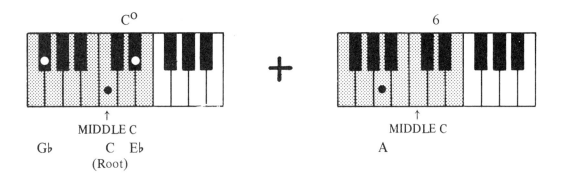

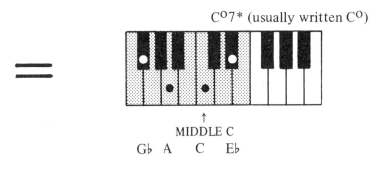

(organ pedal plays "C")

*The apparent contradiction in the NAME of the chord — C^o7 instead of C^o6 — is a throwback to "traditional" harmony and need not concern us here, since for practical purposes the "Diminished 7th" and the "6th" are the same note.

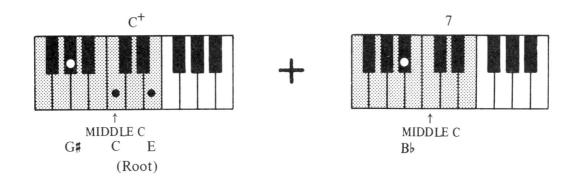

C^+

7

MIDDLE C

G♯   C   E

(Root)

MIDDLE C

B♭

$C7^+$ (sometimes written C^+7)

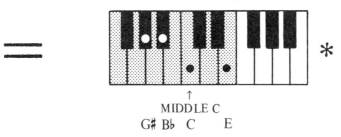

MIDDLE C

G♯ B♭ C   E

*

(organ pedal plays "C")

Exercise 9. Find the following four-note chords (check your UPR and include organ pedals. On piano play chords with either hand):—

a) C♯°

b) B♭°

        (check for similarity between a) and b))

c) F°

d) G7⁺

e) F7⁺

(Answers on page 96)

* This particular "7⁺" combination sounds rather "cluttered" (some do, some don't). If in doubt abandon the "7" and play simply "C^+" (see first Chord Diagram on this page).

SECTION SEVEN   QUICK METHOD FOR FINDING FOUR-NOTE DIMINISHED CHORDS:—

1. Extend Diminished half step formula to:
   3 — 3 — 3

2. With Diminished Chords you may count your half steps in EITHER DIRECTION from the Root to suit the UPR (Usual Playing Range).

Examples:—

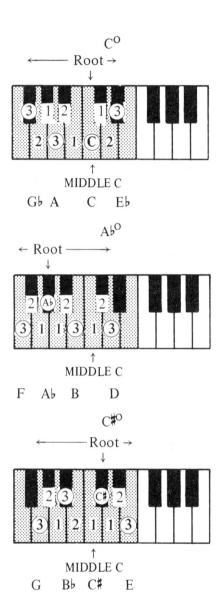

For practical purposes the above three Diminished chords are the only ones you need learn, since all other Diminished chords are the same EXCEPT FOR THE NAMES:—

$$C^O = F\sharp(G\flat)^O = A^O = E\flat(D\sharp)^O$$

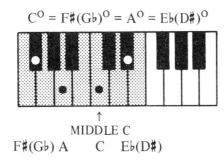

(Play appropriate organ pedal in each case.)

MIDDLE C

F♯(G♭) A   C   E♭(D♯)

$$A\flat(G\sharp)^O = F^O = B^O = D^O$$

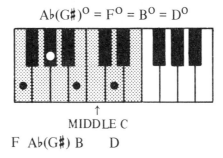

(Play appropriate organ pedal in each case.)

MIDDLE C

F A♭(G♯) B   D

$$C\sharp(D\flat)^O = G^O = B\flat(A\sharp)^O = E^O$$

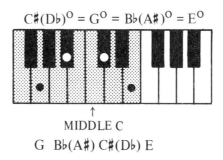

(Play appropriate organ pedal in each case.)

MIDDLE C

G B♭(A♯) C♯(D♭) E

Exercise 10.   Using the "Quick Method" find the following four-note Diminished chords (check your UPR as you go. Include pedals on organ and play chords with either hand on piano):—

         a)   B^O
         b)   G^O
         c)   D^O
         d)   A^O
         e)   E♭^{O}

(Answers on page 96)

SECTION EIGHT   CHORD PROGRESSIONS (2)
Featuring DIMINISHED and AUGMENTED chords

Progression 1:–   C6 – C⁰ – Dm7 – G7 – C6

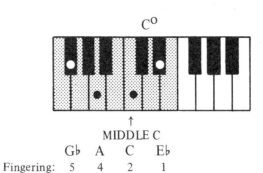

C⁰

MIDDLE C

	Gb	A	C	Eb
Fingering:	5	4	2	1

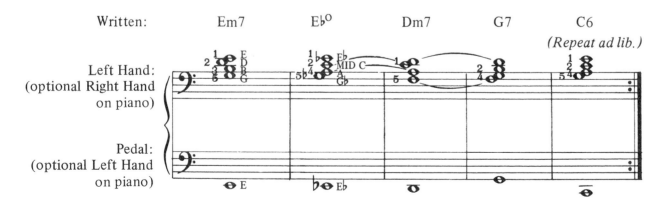

Progression 2:–   Em7 – Eb⁰ – Dm7 – G7 – C6

Eb⁰ = C⁰ (see Progression 1.)

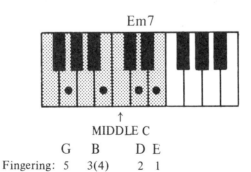

Em7

MIDDLE C

	G	B	D	E
Fingering:	5	3(4)	2	1

24

Progression 3:—   C6 — C#° — Dm7 — G7 — C6

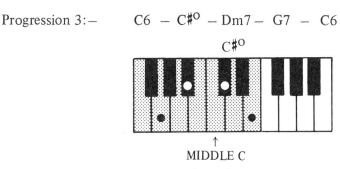

C#°

↑
MIDDLE C

	G	Bb	C#	E
Fingering:	5	3	2	1

Written: C6   C#°   Dm7   G7

(Repeat ad lib.)

Left Hand:
(optional Right Hand
on piano)

Pedal:
(optional Left Hand
on piano)

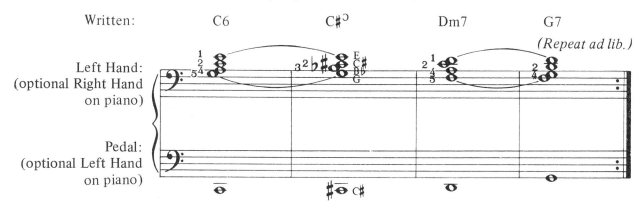

Progression 4:—   C — C⁺ — F6 — G7 — C6

Simple basic three-note chords can sometimes convey a nice feeling of "movement":—

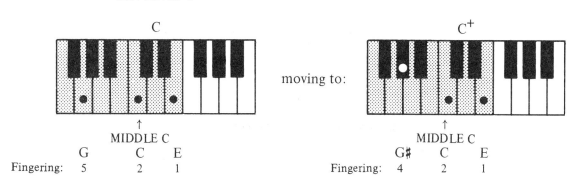

	C			C⁺
--------------	---		--------------	----
↑ MIDDLE C		moving to:	↑ MIDDLE C	

	G	C	E
Fingering:	5	2	1

	G#	C	E
Fingering:	4	2	1

Written:

C   C⁺   F6   G7   C6

(Repeat ad lib.)

Left Hand:
(optional Right Hand
on piano)

Pedal:
(optional Left Hand
on piano)

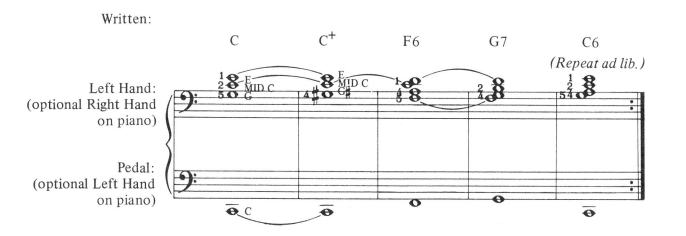

Progression 5:—   C6 — Am7 — Dm7 — G7⁺ — C6

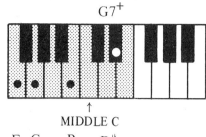

G7⁺

↑
MIDDLE C

	F	G		B		D♯
Fingering:	5	4		2		1

Written:—

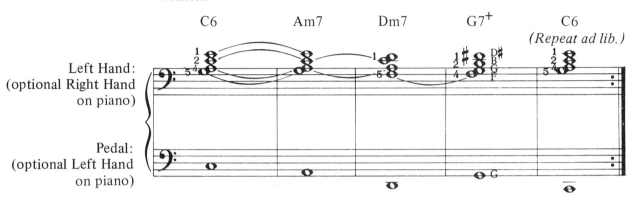

C6   Am7   Dm7   G7⁺   C6
                                                (Repeat ad lib.)

Left Hand:
(optional Right Hand
on piano)

Pedal:
(optional Left Hand
on piano)

Exercise 11.

a) Revise Fm6 (4 notes). Check your UPR.
Play the following Progression (including organ pedals, and playing chords with either hand on piano):—

C — C⁺ — F6 — Fm6 — C6

b) Revise A7 (4 notes). Check your UPR.
Play the following Progression (including pedals, etc.):—

C6 — A7 — Dm7 — G7⁺ — C6

c) Work out and play the following 3-note Progression (including pedals, etc.):—

F — F⁺ — B♭

Check your UPR. The chords should follow one another easily and logically.

d) Play the following Progression (including pedals, etc.):—

F — F⁺ — B♭ — G7⁺ —· C6

The last two chords have FOUR notes each. All chords should be in the UPR.

e) Play the following Progression (including pedals, etc.):—

C6 — C♯º — Dm7 — G7⁺ — C6

(all 4-note chords)

(Answers on page 96)

          ADDED NOTES (3)
The "9", the "–9", and the "+9"

These three "Added Notes" lie ABOVE (i.e. to the RIGHT of) the ROOT:—

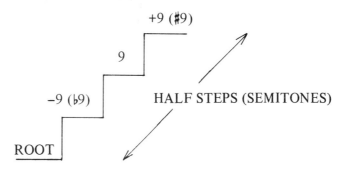

Example 1:   If the ROOT were "C" the three "9's" would be:—

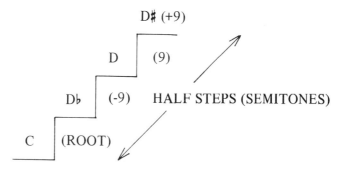

On the keyboard:—

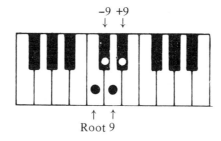

Example 2:   If the ROOT were "B♭" the three "9's" would be:—

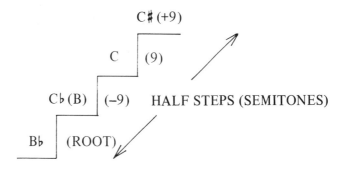

On the keyboard:—

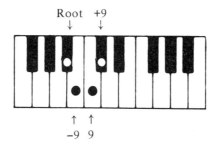

27

Exercise 12.　If the Root were "D", what would be:

　　　　　　　a)　the 9?
　　　　　　　b)　the −9? (sometimes written ♭9, or 9♭)
　　　　　　　c)　the +9? (sometimes written ♯9, or 9♯)

If the Root were "D♭", what would be:

　　　　　　　d)　the −9? (♭9)
　　　　　　　e)　the +9? (♯9)
　　　　　　　f)　the 9?

If the Root were "G", what would be:

　　　　　　　g)　the +9? (♯9)
　　　　　　　h)　the 9?
　　　　　　　i)　the −9? (♭9)

(Answers on page 97)

SECTION TEN   **APPLYING THE "9's" (1)**

RULE: When adding a "9" (or a "−9", or a "+9") to a chord the
ROOT NOTE will actually MOVE to the 9.

Example 1.   Adding a "9" to the chord of "C": −

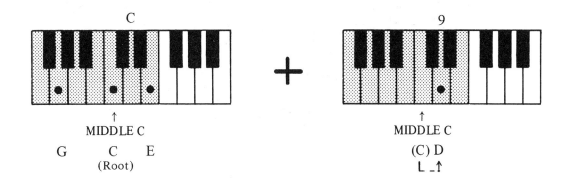

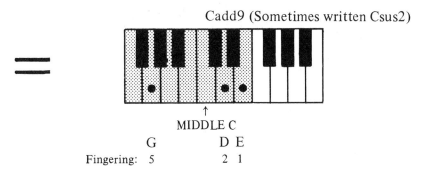

Organ Pedal or piano left hand plays "C" − the missing ROOT NOTE.

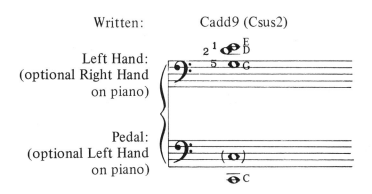

29

Example 2.   Adding a "9" to the chord of "B♭":—

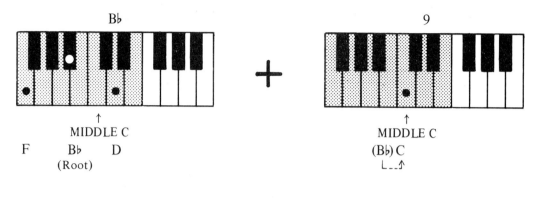

B♭   9

MIDDLE C   MIDDLE C

F   B♭   D   (B♭) C
       (Root)

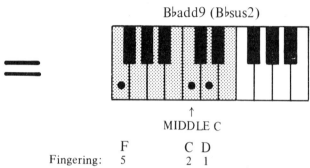

B♭add9 (B♭sus2)

MIDDLE C

                F   C D
Fingering: 5   2 1

Organ Pedal or piano left hand plays "B♭" (Root)

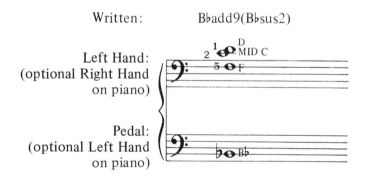

Written: B♭add9(B♭sus2)

Left Hand:
(optional Right Hand
on piano)

Pedal:
(optional Left Hand
on piano)

Exercise 13.   Find the following chords, checking your UPR's in each case,
                 and including organ pedals. (Play chords with either hand on
                 piano):—

                 a)   Fadd 9 (Fsus2)
                 b)   Fm add9 (Fm sus2) (discordant)
                 c)   Cm add9 (Cm sus2) (discordant)
                 d)   Eadd9 (Esus2) In this case place the "9"
                      ABOVE the UPR.
                 e)   Em add9 (Em sus2) Place the "9" ABOVE the
                      UPR.

                 (Answers on page 97)

30

SECTION ELEVEN   APPLYING THE "9's" (2)

It is possible (and quite usual) to add a "9" to a chord that already has four notes, such as:—

C6,   C7,   Cmaj7

These will then become FIVE-NOTE chords including organ pedal (or if using both hands on piano).

Example 1.   Adding a "9" to "C6":—

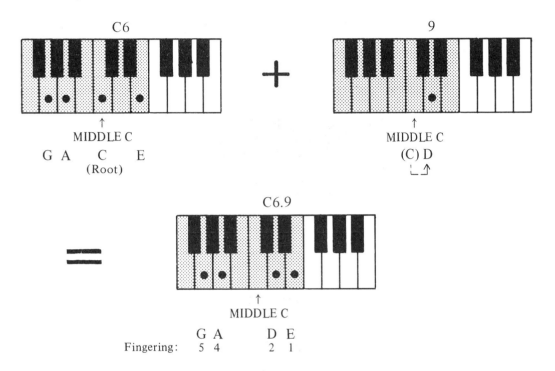

Organ pedal or piano left hand plays "C"

Example 2.   Adding a "9" to "C7":—

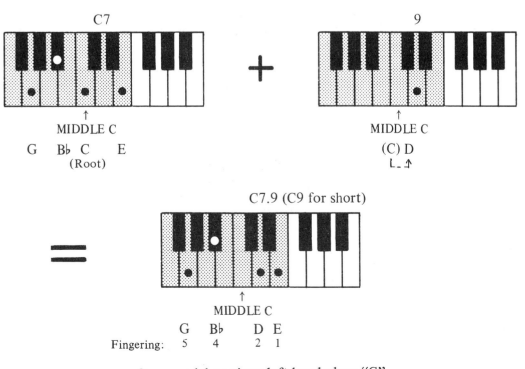

Organ pedal or piano left hand plays "C"

Example 3.   Adding a "9" to "Cmaj7":–

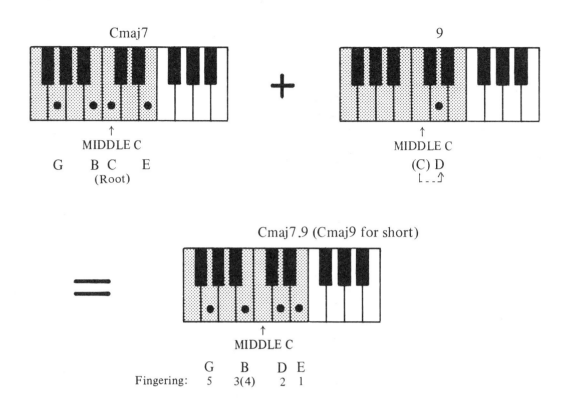

Organ pedal or piano left hand plays "C"

The chords in Examples 1, 2, and 3 written:–

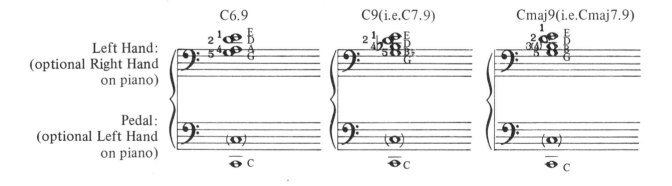

Exercise 14.   Revise B♭6, B♭7, and B♭maj7.
Include organ pedal and check your UPR in each case.
Now find (including organ pedals and playing chords with either hand on piano):—

a)   B♭6.9
b)   B♭9 (i.e. B♭7.9)
c)   B♭maj9 (i.e. B♭maj7.9)

Revise G6, G7, and Gmaj7 (Normal Inversions/Positions)
Include organ pedal and check your UPR in each case.
Now find (include pedals, etc.):—

d)   G9 (i.e. G7.9)
e)   Gmaj9 (i.e. Gmaj7.9)
f)   G6.9

(Answers on page 97)

Exercise 15.   Find the following Minor chords, checking the UPR in each case, and including pedals, etc.

a)   Dm6
b)   Dm6.9
c)   Dm7
d)   Dm9
e)   Dm(maj7)
f)   Dm(maj9)

Find the following Minor chords, going outside the UPR (Usual Playing Range) when instructed. Include pedals, etc.

g)   Em6
h)   Em6.9 (High Inversion)
i)   Em7
j)   Em9 (High Inversion)
k)   Em(maj7) Omit Root from chord to minimize discord.
l)   Em(maj9) (High Inversion)

(Answers on page 97)

SECTION TWELVE   APPLYING THE "−9" AND THE "+9"

These notes can only be added successfully to four-note "7" chords, e.g.:−

C7,   Bb7,   etc.

Furthermore these "7" chords can only be MAJOR.

Example 1.   Adding a "−9" to C7:−

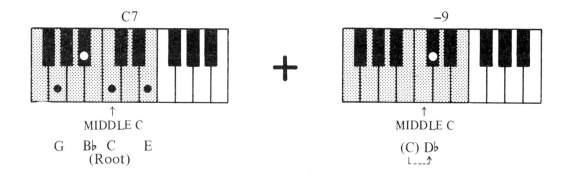

C7   −9

MIDDLE C   MIDDLE C

G   Bb C   E   (C) Db
     (Root)

C7−9* (C−9 for short)

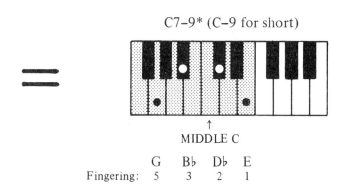

MIDDLE C

           G   Bb   Db   E

Fingering: 5   3   2   1

Organ pedal or piano left hand plays "C"

Written:−

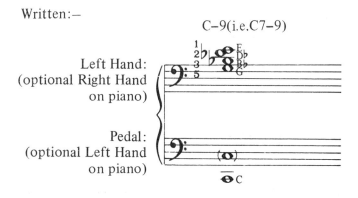

C−9 (i.e. C7−9)

Left Hand:
(optional Right Hand
on piano)

Pedal:
(optional Left Hand
on piano)

*could be written C7^{b9}

34

Example 2.   Adding a "+9" to C7:—

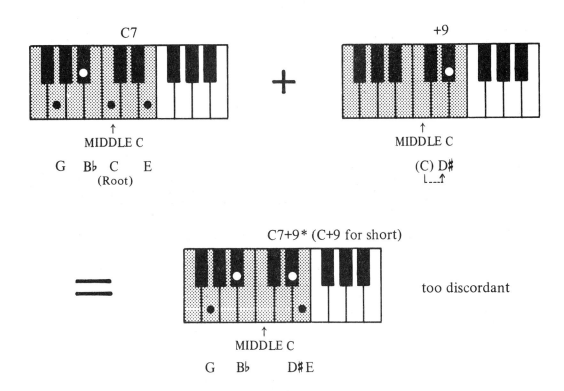

C7

MIDDLE C

G   B♭   C   E
         (Root)

+9

MIDDLE C

(C) D♯
L__↑

C7+9* (C+9 for short)

MIDDLE C

G   B♭   D♯ E

too discordant

Organ pedal or piano left hand plays "C"

C+9 in the above form is too discordant for ordinary use, but the chord can be Inverted as follows (going just outside the UPR):—

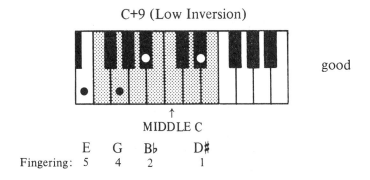

C+9 (Low Inversion)

MIDDLE C

good

         E   G   B♭   D♯
Fingering: 5   4   2   1

Organ pedal or piano left hand plays "C"

The note "G" may be omitted from the above chord if desired, in order to gain clarity:—

*could be written C7♯9

35

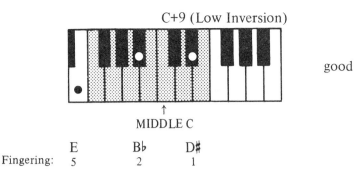

C+9 (Low Inversion)

good

↑
MIDDLE C

Fingering:
E	Bb	D#
5	2	1

Organ pedal or piano left hand plays "C"

The chord(s) written:—

*

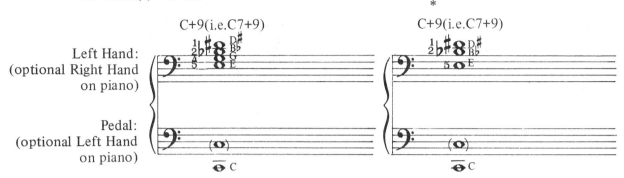

C+9(i.e.C7+9)   C+9(i.e.C7+9)

Left Hand:
(optional Right Hand
on piano)

Pedal:
(optional Left Hand
on piano)

Exercise 16.   Find the following 4-note chords. Check your UPR in each case. Include Pedal (the 5th note). Play chords with either hand on piano:—

a) Bb–9 (i.e. Bb7–9)
b) G–9 (i.e. G7–9)
c) What is the difference between a) and b)?
d) D–9 (i.e. D7–9)
e) A–9 (i.e. A7–9)

(Answers on page 97)

Exercise 17.   a) Revise D7, then find:—
D$^+$9 (i.e. D7$^+$9 – 4 notes)
Go ABOVE the UPR. Include Pedal (the 5th note).

b) By omitting note "A" from above chord play:—
D$^+$9 (3 notes)
Include Pedal. This is the more usual form of the chord.

c) Find Db7. Check your UPR. Include Pedal.
d) Find:
Db$^+$9 (i.e. Db7$^+$9 – 4 notes)
Check your UPR. Include Pedal.

e) By omitting note "Ab" from above chord play:—
Db$^+$9 (3 notes)
Include Pedal. This is the more usual form of the chord.

f) Find Eb7. Check your UPR. Include Pedal.

g) Find:—
Eb$^+$9 (i.e. Eb7$^+$9 – 4 notes)
Go ABOVE the UPR. Include Pedal.

h) By omitting note "Bb" from above chord play:—
Eb$^+$9 (3 notes)
Include Pedal. This is the more usual form of the chord.

* The more usual version: three notes plus organ pedal (or piano left hand)

(Answers on page 97)

36

All "–9" chords are the same as DIMINISHED chords except for the ROOT
NOTE.

Example:–

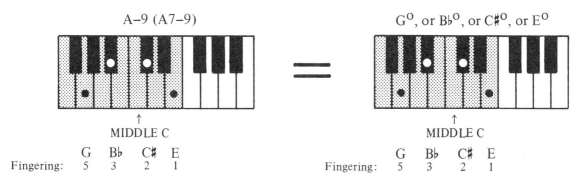

Organ pedal (piano left hand) plays   Organ pedal (piano left hand) plays
"A" (ROOT)   "G", "Bb", "C♯", or "E" (ROOTS)

Progression 1:–   C6 – A⁻⁹ – Dm7 – G7 – C6

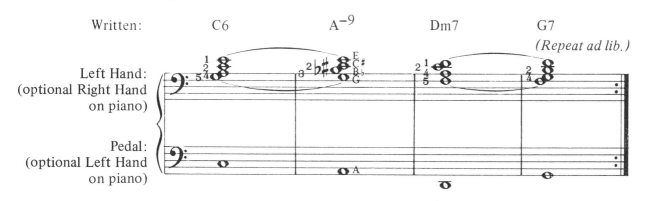

Progression 2:–   Am7 – D⁻⁹ – Dm7 – G7 – C6

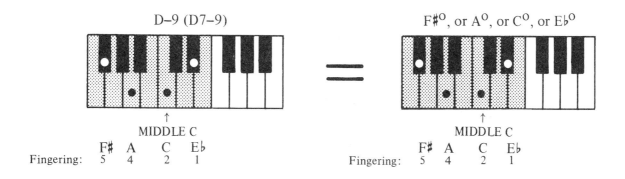

Organ pedal (piano left hand) plays   Organ pedal (piano left hand) plays
"D" (ROOT)   "F♯", "A", "C", or "Eb" (ROOTS)

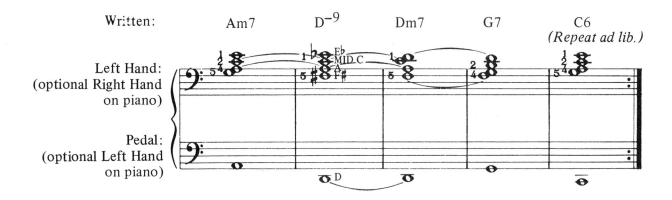

Progression 3:—   C+9 – F6

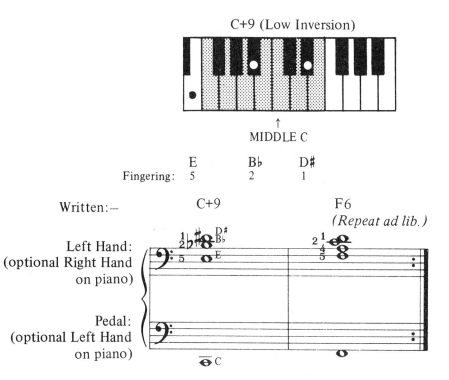

Progression 4:—   G7 – C+9 – Fmaj7

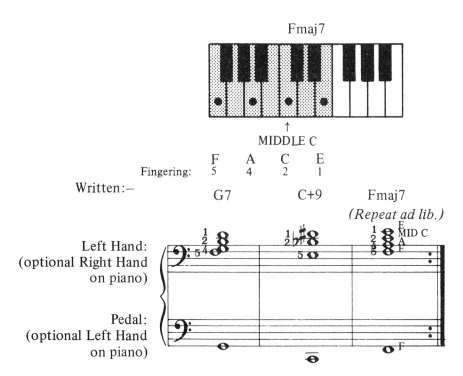

Progression 5:—   Fmaj7 – D⁺9 – G7 – C⁺9 – Fmaj7

D+9 (High Inversion)

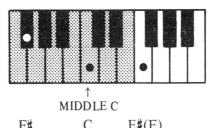

↑
MIDDLE C

	F♯	C	E♯(F)
Fingering:	5	2	1

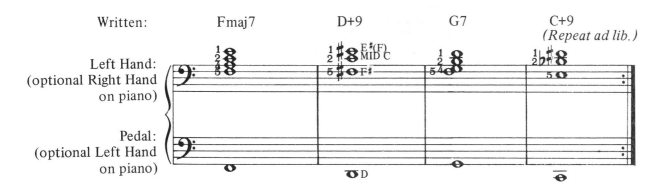

Exercise 18.   Having revised chords as necessary, play the following
Chord Progressions (including organ pedals, and playing
chords with either hand on piano):—

a)   Fmaj7 – D⁻9 – Dm7 – G7 – C6
b)   Dm7 – G⁻9 – C6
c)   Dm7 – G⁻9 – Cmaj7 – C6
d)   Fmaj7 – D⁻9 – Dm7 – G⁻9 – Cmaj7 – C6
e)   Gm7 (Normal Inversion) – C⁺9 – Fmaj7 – F6
f)   Am7 – D⁺9 – Gm7 (Normal Inversion) – C⁺9
        – Fmaj7
g)   Cmaj7 – Am7 – D⁺9 – G⁻9 – C6

(Answers on pages 97 and 98)

SECTION FOURTEEN   CHORD PROGRESSIONS (4)
Featuring "9's" in general

Progression 1:—   Cadd9 — C — Dm7 — G7 — C6

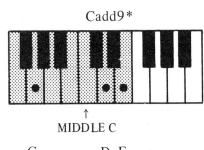

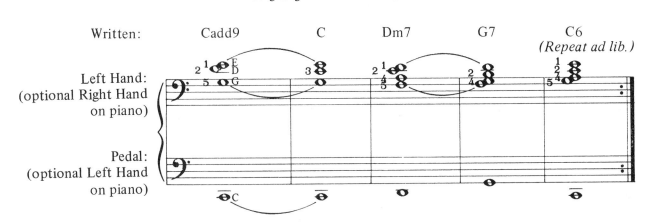

Progression 2:—   Cm^add9 — Cm — Fm6 — G7 — Cm6

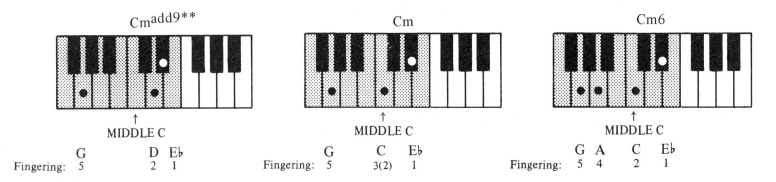

*could be written: C^sus2
**could be written: Cm^sus2

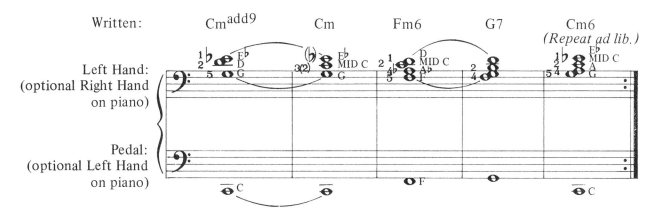

Progression 3:—   C6.9 — Am7 — Dm7 — G7 — C6

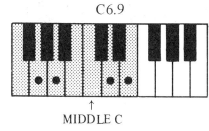

MIDDLE C

	G	A		D	E
Fingering:	5	4		2	1

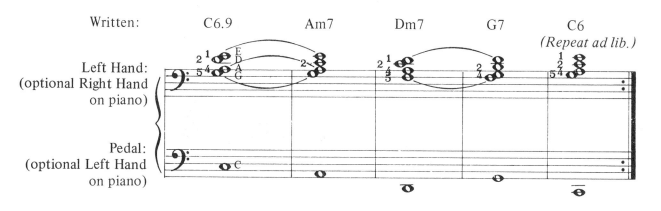

Progression 4:—   C6.9 — C9 — F6 — G7 — C6

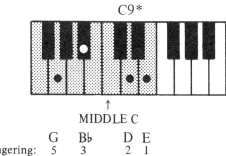

MIDDLE C

	G	Bb		D	E
Fingering:	5	3		2	1

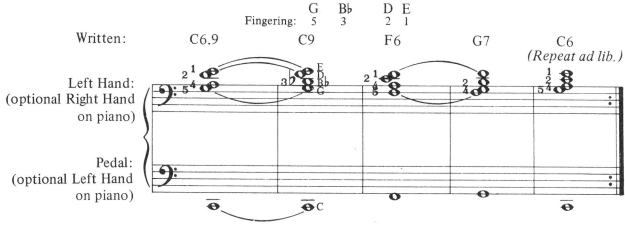

41

*i.e. C7.9

Progression 5:—   Cmaj9 — C9 — F6 — G7 — C6

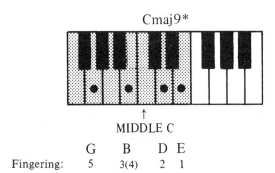

MIDDLE C

	G	B	D	E
Fingering:	5	3(4)	2	1

Written:

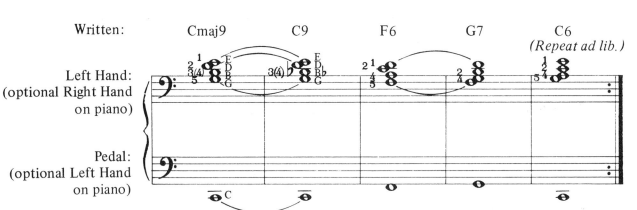

Exercise 19.   Play the following Progressions. (Include organ pedals. Play chords with either hand on piano):—

a)   Cmaj9 — Am7 — Dm7 — G7 — C6
b)   C6.9 — A7 — Dm7 — G7 — C6
c)   C6 — C9 — F6 — Fm6 — C6
d)   Cadd9 — C — Fmaj7 — Fm6 — Cmaj7

Revise G9 and G^{-9}, then play:—

e)   Cm^{add9} — Cm — D7 — G^{-9} — Cm6
f)   Cmaj9 — C6 — G9 — G^{-9} — C6

Find D9, revise Dm9, then play:—

g)   Cmaj9 — Am7 — Dm9 — G^{-9} — C6
h)   Cmaj9 — A^{-9} — D9 — G^{-9} — Cmaj7

(Answers on page 98)

*i.e. Cmaj7.9

SECTION FIFTEEN   **THE "SUS 4"**

The scale of C consists of seven "white" notes:—

Scale of C

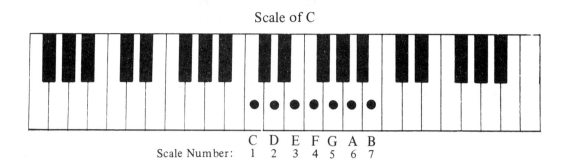

```
                     C  D  E  F  G  A  B
Scale Number:        1  2  3  4  5  6  7
```

Looking again at the Chord of C (original basic version, NOT in the UPR):—

C (Root Position)*

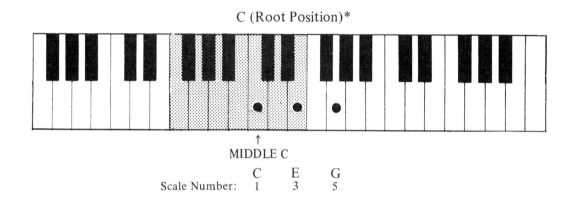

```
                     ↑
                  MIDDLE C
                  C     E     G
Scale Number:     1     3     5
```

The Chord of C (illustrated above) consists of:—

       Number 1 of the Scale
       Number 3 of the Scale
       Number 5 of the Scale
all played together.

Number 1 of the Scale (called the "Root" when used in a chord) cannot be altered.

Number 3 of the Scale (called the "3rd" when used in a chord) CAN be altered (one half step either way).

Number 5 of the Scale (called the "5th" when used in a chord) CAN be altered (one half step either way).

*i.e. The ROOT (C) is the BOTTOM NOTE of the chord.

In this SECTION we are interested in:—

The "3rd" (Number 3 of the Scale)

If the "3rd" in the chord of C is played one half step LOWER the chord changes from Major to Minor:—

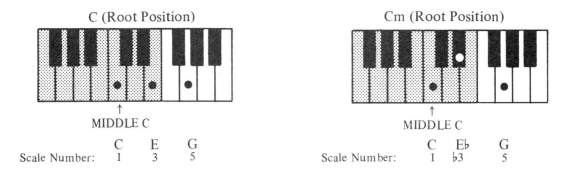

If the "3rd" in the chord of C is played one half step HIGHER it will become the "4th" of the Scale, and the resulting mild discord is called "C SUSPENDED 4th" (Csus4, or Csus, for short):—

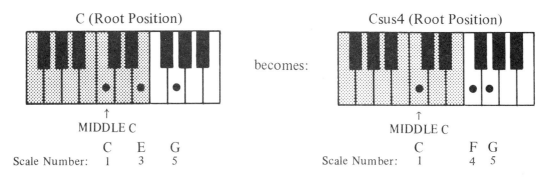

Since at present Csus4 is inconveniently placed (i.e. it is too high), we will Invert it (i.e. alter the ORDER of the notes) as follows:—

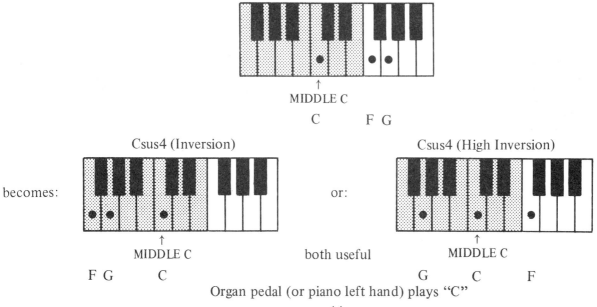

Organ pedal (or piano left hand) plays "C"

44

METHOD FOR FINDING AND PLACING "SUS 4" CHORDS:–

Example 1.   AIM: To find Gsus4 and place it correctly.

a)   Find the chord of "G":–

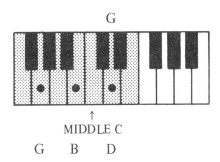

This chord is already correctly placed in the UPR.

b)   Decide which of the three notes above is the "3rd".

The notes of any basic chord always appear in the same order:–

ROOT $\longrightarrow$ 3rd $\longrightarrow$ 5th

In the above example:–

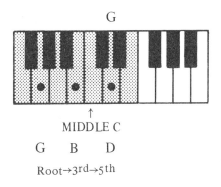

So "B" is the "3rd".

c)   Move the 3rd up ONE half step (Major Chords) or TWO half steps (Minor Chords) to the 4th:–

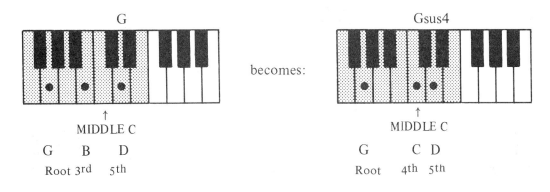

becomes:

Organ pedal (or piano left hand) plays "G"

45

Example 2.   AIM: To find B♭sus4 and place it correctly.

a)   Find the chord of B♭:—

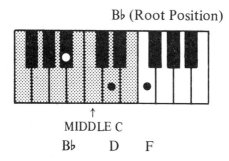

B♭ (Root Position)

↑
MIDDLE C
B♭   D   F

The chord is too high, so drop the top note (F) one octave:—

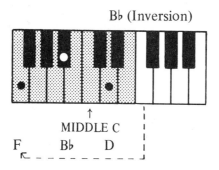

B♭ (Inversion)

↑
MIDDLE C
F   B♭   D

The chord is now correctly placed (in the UPR).

b)   Decide which of the three notes above is the "3rd".

ROOT ⟶ 3rd ⟶ 5th

Expressed "circularly":—

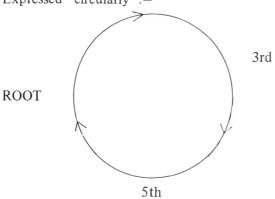

ROOT

3rd

5th

Applied to the above example:—

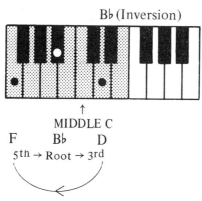

B♭ (Inversion)

↑
MIDDLE C
F   B♭   D
5th → Root → 3rd

So "D" is the "3rd".

46

c) Move the 3rd up ONE half step (Major Chord) to the 4th: —

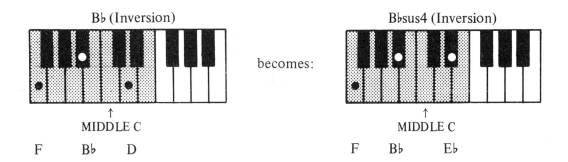

Bb (Inversion)   becomes: Bbsus4 (Inversion)

MIDDLE C   MIDDLE C

F   Bb   D   F   Bb   Eb

Organ pedal (or piano left hand) plays "Bb"

Exercise 20.   Find the following chords. Check your UPR in each case. (Include organ pedals. Play chords with either hand on piano): —

a) Fsus4
b) Asus4
c) Dsus4
d) Esus4
e) E sus4

(answers on page 98)

SECTION SIXTEEN CHORD PROGRESSIONS (5)
Featuring "Sus 4's"

Progression 1:— Csus4 — C — Dm7 — G7 — C6

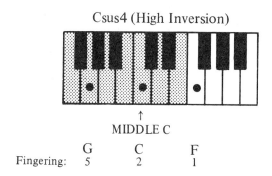

Csus4 (High Inversion)

↑
MIDDLE C

	G	C	F
Fingering:	5	2	1

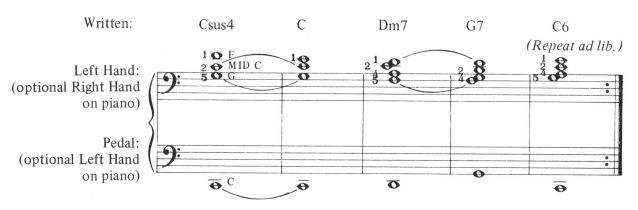

Progression 2:— Csus4 — C — Gsus4 — G — C

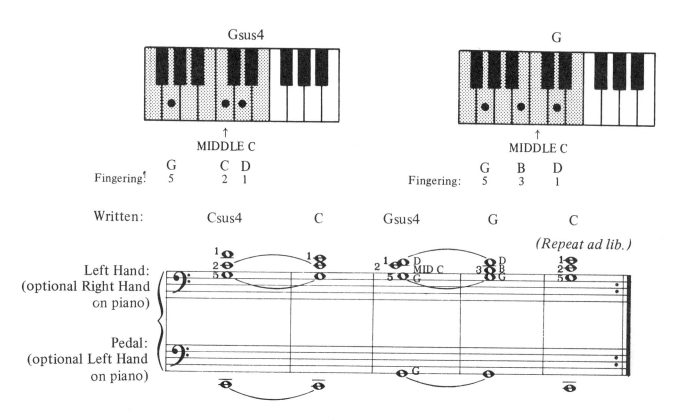

The above is a typical "Hymn" progression, but "sus 4" chords are used also in many "Popular" Music categories, such as "Folk", "Country", "Rock", etc.

Progression 3:—   Fsus4 — F — Gsus4 — G — Cadd9 — C

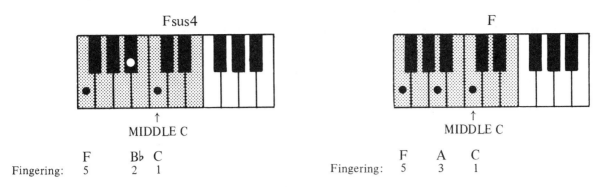

Fsus4

MIDDLE C

	F	B♭	C
Fingering:	5	2	1

F

MIDDLE C

	F	A	C
Fingering:	5	3	1

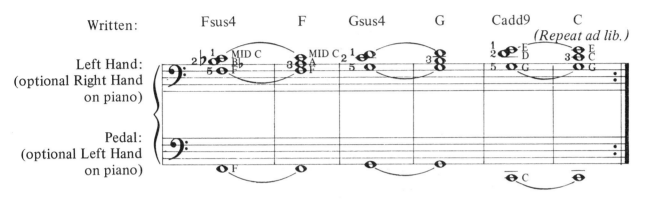

Written: Fsus4   F   Gsus4   G   Cadd9   C

(Repeat ad lib.)

Left Hand:
(optional Right Hand
on piano)

Pedal:
(optional Left Hand
on piano)

Exercise 21.   Having revised chords as necessary, play the following Progressions. (Include organ pedals. Play chords with either hand
on piano):—

a)   B♭sus4 — B♭ — Gsus4 — G — C
b)   Csus4 (High Inversion) — B♭sus4 — Gsus4 — G —
     C
c)   Fsus4 — F — Gsus4 — G — Asus4 — A
d)   B♭sus4 — B♭ — Csus4 (High Inversion) — C —
     Dsus4 — D
e)   Fsus4 — F — E♭sus4 — E♭ — Dsus4

(Answers on pages 98 and 99)

49

SECTION SEVENTEEN   THE "SUS 4" WITH MINOR CHORDS

Since it has no "3rd", a chord such as:—

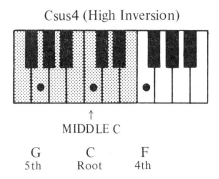

Csus4 (High Inversion)

↑
MIDDLE C

G	C	F
5th	Root	4th

is neither Major nor Minor.

However when the above chord is followed by its own MINOR chord (or if C MINOR rather than C MAJOR is being somehow implied) the chord is called "Cm sus4".

Example:—   Cm sus4 – Cm – Gsus4 – G – Cm

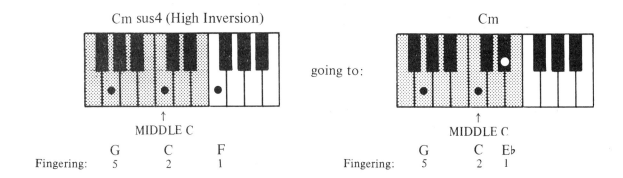

Cm sus4 (High Inversion)   Cm

going to:

↑   ↑
MIDDLE C   MIDDLE C

	G	C	F			G	C	Eb
--------------	---	---	---		--------------	---	---	----
Fingering:	5	2	1		Fingering:	5	2	1

The above Progression written:—

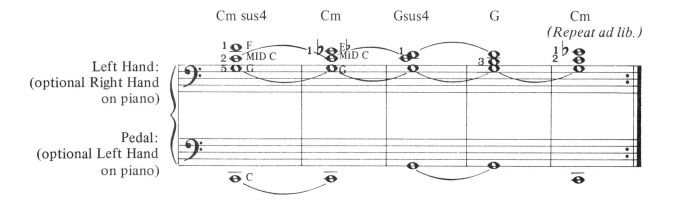

Left Hand:
(optional Right Hand
on piano)

Pedal:
(optional Left Hand
on piano)

50

METHODS FOR FINDING (AND PLACING) "MINOR SUS 4" CHORDS,
e.g. "Gm sus4":

METHOD 1.   Since for practical purposes:

$$Gm^{sus4} = G^{sus4}$$

we could ignore the "Minor" aspect of the chord and work
out "Gsus4" (the Major version) instead (see page 45).

METHOD 2.   (Based on the Method given on page 45)

    a)   Find G Minor and place it correctly (i.e. in the UPR)
    b)   Decide which of the three notes is the "3rd".
    c)   Since the basic chord is Minor (i.e. G Minor) move
        the 3rd up TWO half steps to the right so that it
        becomes the "4th".

Result (using either Method):–

Gm^{sus4} (same as G^{sus4}, but "implying" G Minor here)

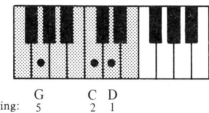

Fingering:
G	C	D
5	2	1

Organ pedal (or piano left hand) plays "G"

Exercise 22.   Having found (or revised) the necessary chords, play the
following Progressions. (Include organ pedals. Play chords
with either hand on piano):–

    a)   Cm sus4 (High Inversion) – Cm – Fm6 – G7
          – Cm6
    b)   Gm sus4 – Gm – Fm sus4 – Fm – Gsus4 – G
    c)   Am sus4 – Am – Gm sus4 – Gm – A
    d)   Am sus4 – Am – Asus4 – A – Dsus4 – D
    e)   Cm sus4 (High Inversion) – Cm – Gm sus4 – Gm
          – Asus4

(Answers on page 99)

SECTION EIGHTEEN   "SUS 4's" AND "7's"

The only ADDED NOTE commonly used with "sus 4" chords is the "7"*:—

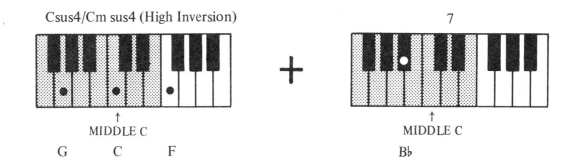

Csus4/Cm sus4 (High Inversion)

MIDDLE C

G   C   F

7

MIDDLE C

B♭

＋

＝

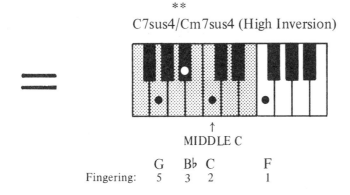

**
C7sus4/Cm7sus4 (High Inversion)

MIDDLE C

	G	B♭	C		F
Fingering:	5	3	2		1

Organ pedal (or piano left hand) plays "C"

Progression 1:—   F6 − Dm7 − C7sus4 (High Inversion) − C7 − F6

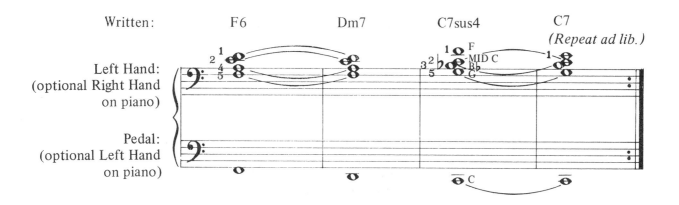

Written: F6   Dm7   C7sus4   C7
(Repeat ad lib.)

Left Hand:
(optional Right Hand
on piano)

Pedal:
(optional Left Hand
on piano)

*The "9" is also used with this combination, but in such a case the "sus4" chord would become an "11th" chord (see SECTION TWENTY TWO, p.68)

** Often written: C7sus/Cm7sus

52

Progression 2:– Cm7^sus4 (High Inversion) – Cm7 – F7^sus4 – F7 – B♭6

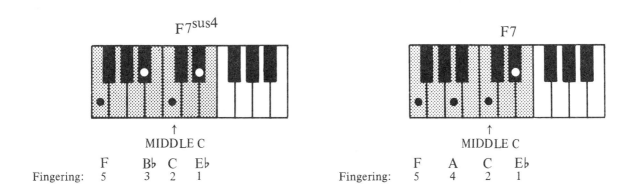

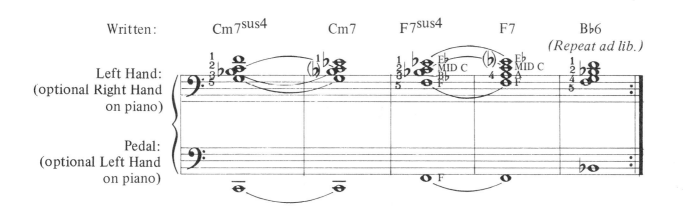

Exercise 23.   Find:–

        a)   G7sus4 (G7sus)
        b)   Gm7sus4 (Gm7sus)
        c)   D7sus4 (D7sus)
        d)   Fm7sus4 (Fm7sus)
        e)   A7sus4 (A7sus)

(Answers on page 99)

Exercise 24.   Revise or find chords as necessary to play the following Progressions. (Include organ pedals. Play chords with either hand on piano.):–

        a)   C6 – Am7 – G7sus – G7 – C6
        b)   D7sus – D7 – G7sus – G7 – Cmaj7
        c)   Gm7sus – Gm7 – C7sus (High Inversion) – C7
              – Fmaj7
        d)   Am7sus – Am7 – D7sus – G^{-9} – C6
        e)   A7sus – A7 – D7sus – D7 – G6

(Answers on pages 99 and 100)

The Scale of C again:—

Scale of C

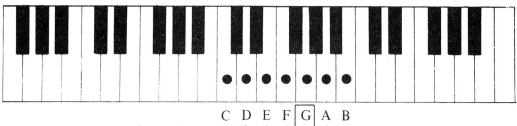

	C	D	E	F	G	A	B
scale number:	1	2	3	4	5	6	7

The Chord of C again:

C (Root Position)

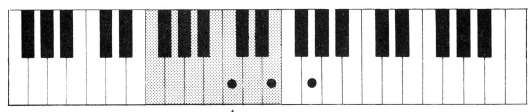

↑
MIDDLE C

	C	E	G
scale number:	1	3	5

"G" is the "5th" note of the SCALE of C.
"G" is the "5th" in the CHORD of C.

The "5th" of any chord may be altered (one half step either way).

When the "5th" is RAISED by one half step the following chord is created:—

C⁺5* (C⁺) (C Augmented)

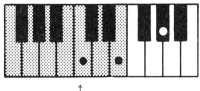

↑
MIDDLE C

	C	E	G♯
scale number:	1	3	♯5

* Could be written: C♯5

54

When the 5th is LOWERED by one half step the following chord is created:—

C–5*

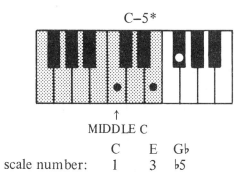

↑
MIDDLE C

	C	E	G♭
scale number:	1	3	♭5

Since at present the above two chords are not in the UPR (Usual Playing Range) we will Invert them (i.e. alter the ORDER of the notes) as follows:—

C+5 (Root Position)   C+5 (Inversion)

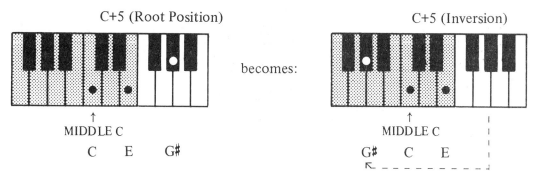

becomes:

↑   ↑
MIDDLE C   MIDDLE C

C   E   G♯   G♯   C   E

Organ pedal (piano left hand) plays "C"

C–5 (Root Position)   C–5 (Inversion)

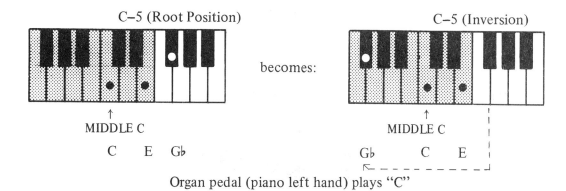

becomes:

↑   ↑
MIDDLE C   MIDDLE C

C   E   G♭   G♭   C   E

Organ pedal (piano left hand) plays "C"

METHOD FOR FINDING "+5" AND "–5" CHORDS

Example 1.   AIM: To find G+5 and G–5 and to place the two chords correctly (i.e. conveniently).

a)   Find "G":—

G (Root Position)

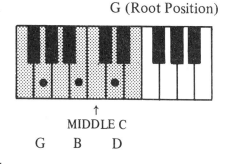

↑
MIDDLE C

G   B   D

* Could be written: C♭5

55

This chord is already conveniently placed in the UPR.

     b)   Decide which of the three notes is the "5th".

ROOT ⟶ 3rd ⟶ 5th

Applying this rule to the present example:—

G

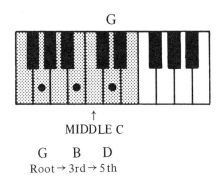

MIDDLE C

G   B   D

Root → 3rd → 5th

"D" is the "5th".

     c)   Move the "5th" UP one half step to form "G+5":—

G+5 (G+) (G Augmented)

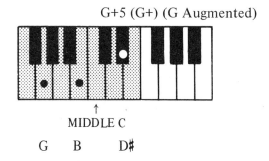

MIDDLE C

G   B   D♯

Organ pedal (piano left hand) plays "G"

Move the "5th" DOWN one half step to form "G–5":—

G–5

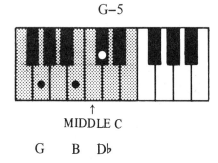

MIDDLE C

G   B   D♭

Organ pedal (piano left hand) plays "G"

Example 2.   AIM: To find Bb+5 and Bb−5 and to place the two chords correctly (i.e. conveniently).

a)   Find "Bb":−

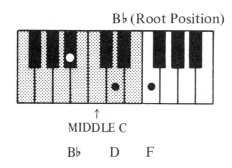

Bb (Root Position)

MIDDLE C

Bb   D   F

This chord is too high, so drop the top note (F) one octave:−

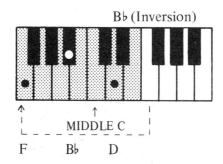

Bb (Inversion)

MIDDLE C

F   Bb   D

The chord is now conveniently placed (in the UPR).

b)   Decide which of the three notes above is the "5th".

ROOT ⟶ 3rd ⟶ 5th

Expressed circularly:−

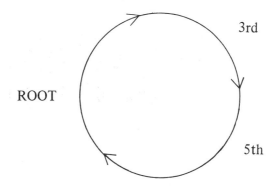

ROOT

3rd

5th

57

Applied to the above example:—

B♭ (Inversion)

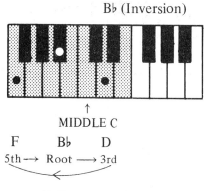

↑
MIDDLE C

F   B♭   D

5th ⟶ Root ⟶ 3rd

"F" is the "5th".

  c) Move the "5th" UP one half step to form "B♭+5":—

B♭+5 (Inversion)

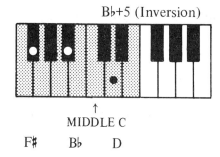

↑
MIDDLE C

F♯   B♭   D

Organ pedal (piano left hand) plays "B♭"

Move the "5th" DOWN one half step to form "B♭−5":—

B♭−5 (Low Inversion)

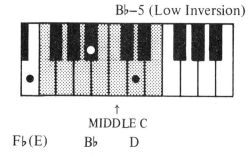

↑
MIDDLE C

F♭(E)   B♭   D

Organ pedal (piano left hand) plays "B♭"

In case this "Low Inversion" of B♭−5 should prove inconvenient (and it sometimes will) we will make a "normal" Inversion of the chord by raising the bottom note (E) one octave:—

58

Bb–5 (Normal Inversion)

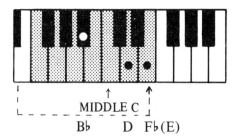

↑
MIDDLE C
Bb   D Fb(E)

Organ pedal (piano left hand) plays "Bb"

Exercise 25.   Find the following chords. Check your UPR in each case. Include organ pedals. Play chords with either hand on piano:—

a)   D+5 (D Augmented)
b)   D–5
c)   A+5 (A Augmented) (High Inversion)
d)   A–5
e)   Cm+5
f)   Cm–5 (C Diminished)

g)   Gm+5
h)   Gm–5 (G Diminished)
i)   Dm+5
j)   Dm–5 (D Diminished)
k)   Am+5 (High Inversion)
l)   Am–5 (A Diminished)

(Answers on page 100)

59

As we have seen, in a simple chord of "C" the "5th" is "G", the "+5" is G♯, the "−5" is G♭:—

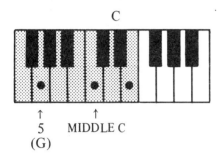

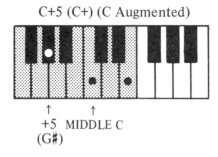

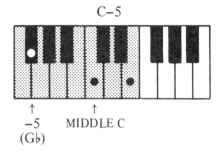

In a chord of "C7" the "5's" will be exactly the same:—

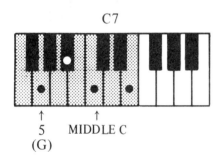

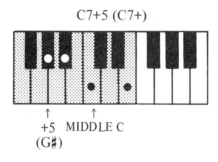

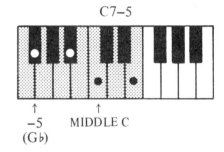

In a chord of "C9" the "5's" will be exactly the same:—

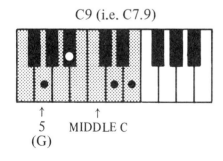

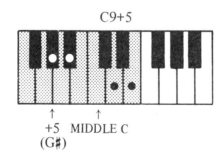

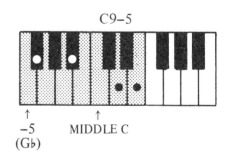

The same applies to all Minor chords, e.g.:—

Cm

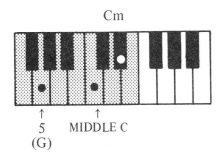

↑
5
(G) MIDDLE C

Cm+5

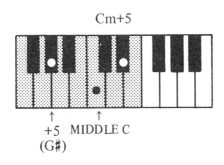

↑
+5 MIDDLE C
(G♯)

Cm−5 (C°)

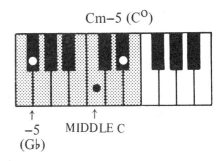

↑
−5 MIDDLE C
(G♭)

Some mixtures, however, are too cluttered or discordant to be of any practical use:—

Cm7

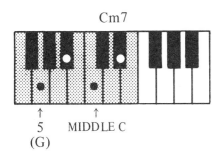

↑
5
(G) MIDDLE C

good

Cm7+5

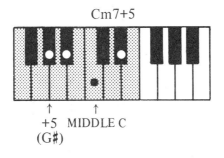

↑
+5 MIDDLE C
(G♯)

too cluttered

Cm7−5*

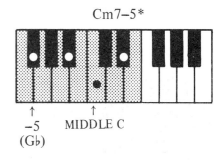

↑
−5 MIDDLE C
(G♭)

good

GENERAL METHOD FOR DEALING WITH COMPLEX "+5" AND "−5" MIXTURES:—

a) Find the basic chord first.
b) Decide which of the notes is the 5th.
c) Alter the 5th accordingly.
d) Add any other notes required.

Example 1. AIM:— To find C−9−5 (i.e. C7−9−5) and place it correctly (i.e. conveniently).

a) The basic chord, placed correctly (in the UPR):—

C (Inversion)

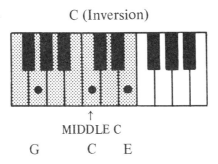

↑
MIDDLE C
G   C   E

* could be written C⌀ (C Half-Diminished)

61

b) Applying:

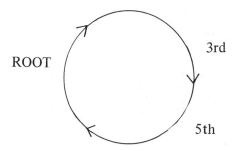

ROOT

3rd

5th

to the above chord:—

C

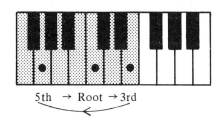

5th → Root →3rd

The 5th is "G"

c) Alter the 5th accordingly:—

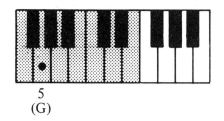

5
(G)

becomes:

−5
(G♭)

C−5

the chord so far:—

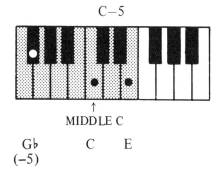

↑
MIDDLE C

G♭   C   E
(−5)

d) Add the "7":—

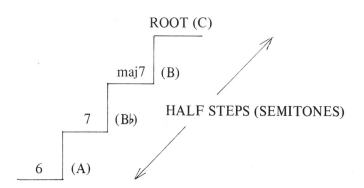

ROOT (C)

maj7 | (B)

7 | (B♭)

HALF STEPS (SEMITONES)

6 | (A)

62

The "7" in this case is "Bb":—

C7–5

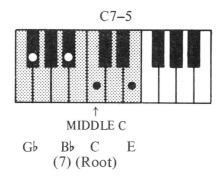

↑
MIDDLE C

Gb   Bb   C   E
     (7) (Root)

Add the "–9":—

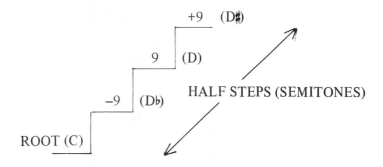

+9 (D#)

9 (D)

–9 (Db)

HALF STEPS (SEMITONES)

ROOT (C)

The "–9" in this case is "Db".

As in all "9" chords (RULE, SECTION TEN, page 29) the Root note will actually MOVE to the "9" (or "–9", or "+9").

So here "C" (The Root) will MOVE to "Db" (–9):—

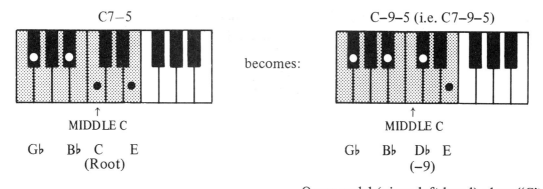

C7–5   C–9–5 (i.e. C7–9–5)

becomes:

↑   ↑
MIDDLE C   MIDDLE C

Gb   Bb   C   E   Gb   Bb   Db   E
     (Root)   (–9)

Organ pedal (piano left hand) plays "C"

Example 2.   AIM:— To find G9+5 (i.e. G7.9+5)

a)   G

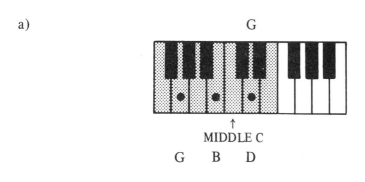

↑
MIDDLE C

G   B   D

b)

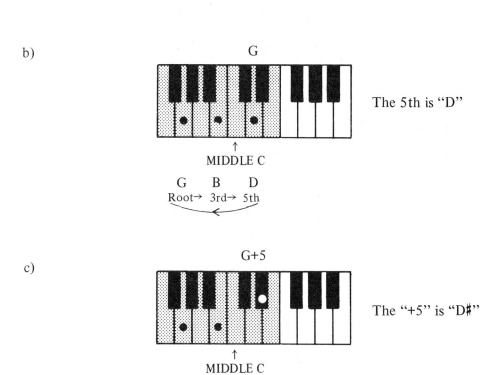

G

The 5th is "D"

MIDDLE C

G B D
Root→ 3rd→ 5th

c)

G+5

The "+5" is "D♯"

MIDDLE C

G B D♯
   (+5)

d)

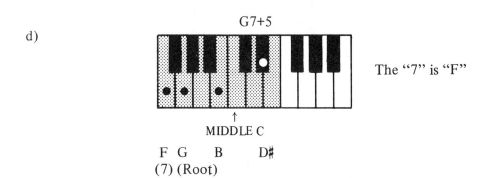

G7+5

The "7" is "F"

MIDDLE C

F G B D♯
(7) (Root)

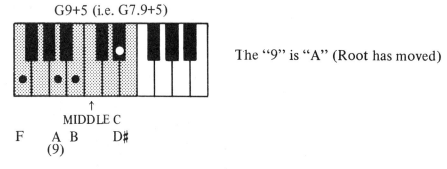

G9+5 (i.e. G7.9+5)

The "9" is "A" (Root has moved)

MIDDLE C

F A B D♯
 (9)

Organ pedal (piano left hand) plays "G" (Root)

Exercise 26. Using the GENERAL METHOD employed above, find the following chords. (Include organ pedals. Play chords with either hand on piano):—

a) Gm7–5 (G$^{\phi}$)

b) Gm7–5 (G$^{\phi}$) (High Inversion)

c) G7–5

d) D7–5

e) Am7–5 (A$^{\phi}$)

f) B7–5

g) D9+5

h) A9+5 (High Inversion)

i) A–9+5 (High Inversion)

j) G–9+5

k) F–9–5

l) E–9–5

(Answers on page 100)

64

Progression 1:—   Cmaj7 − C7^{-5} − Fmaj7 − Fm6 − Cmaj7

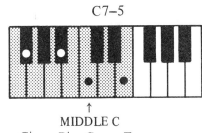

C7−5

MIDDLE C

	Gb	Bb	C	E
Fingering:	5	3	2	1

Written: Cmaj7   C7−5   Fmaj7   Fm6

(Repeat ad lib.)

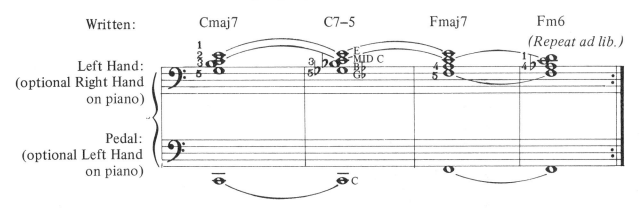

Left Hand:
(optional Right Hand
on piano)

Pedal:
(optional Left Hand
on piano)

Progression 2:—   G7 (High) − Gm7^{-5} (High) − C9 − C^{-9-5} − F6

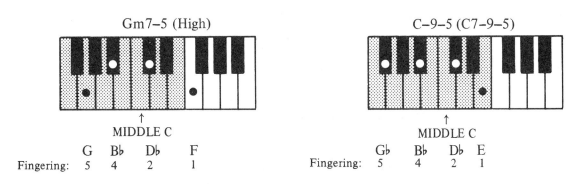

Gm7−5 (High)   C−9−5 (C7−9−5)

MIDDLE C   MIDDLE C

	G	Bb	Db	F			Gb	Bb	Db	E
Fingering:	5	4	2	1		Fingering:	5	4	2	1

Written: G7   Gm7−5   C9   C−9−5   F6

(Repeat ad lib.)

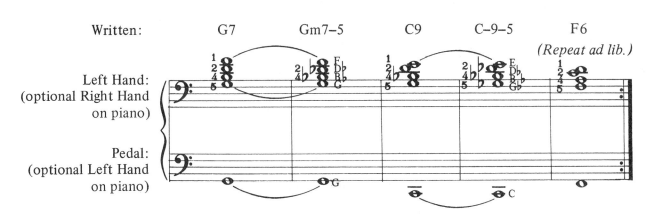

Left Hand:
(optional Right Hand
on piano)

Pedal:
(optional Left Hand
on piano)

65

Progression 3:— Am7 — D9+5 — G9 — G9+5 — Cmaj7

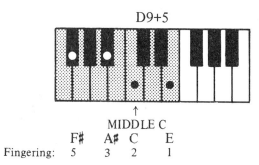

D9+5

MIDDLE C

F♯	A♯	C	E
Fingering: 5 | 3 | 2 | 1

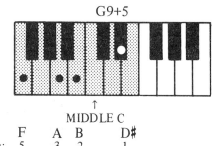

G9+5

MIDDLE C

F	A	B	D♯
Fingering: 5 | 3 | 2 | 1

Written:

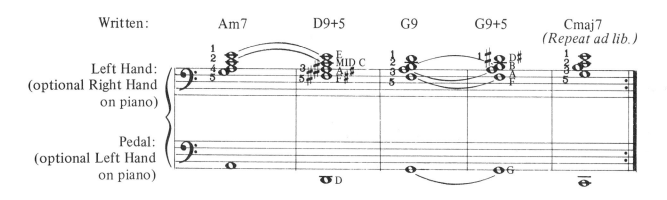

Left Hand:
(optional Right Hand
on piano)

Pedal:
(optional Left Hand
on piano)

Progression 4:— Am7^{-5} — D^{-9} — Dm7^{-5} — G^{-9} — Cmaj9

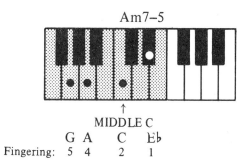

Am7−5

MIDDLE C

G	A	C	E♭
Fingering: 5 | 4 | 2 | 1

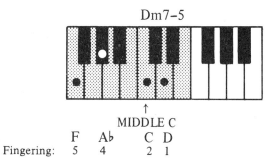

Dm7−5

MIDDLE C

F	A♭	C	D
Fingering: 5 | 4 | 2 | 1

Written:

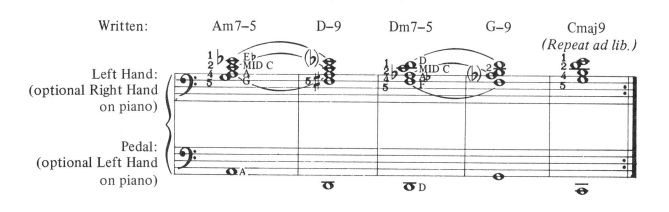

Left Hand:
(optional Right Hand
on piano)

Pedal:
(optional Left Hand
on piano)

66

Progression 5:—   Em7 — A9+5 (High Inversion) — A^{-9}+5 (High Inversion) — A^{-9} — D7

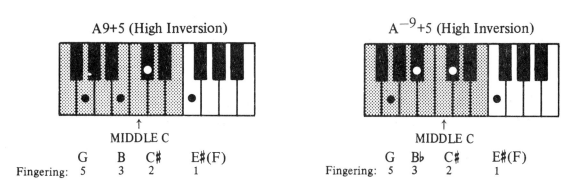

A9+5 (High Inversion)

MIDDLE C

	G	B	C#	E#(F)
Fingering:	5	3	2	1

A^{-9}+5 (High Inversion)

MIDDLE C

	G	B♭	C#	E#(F)
Fingering:	5	3	2	1

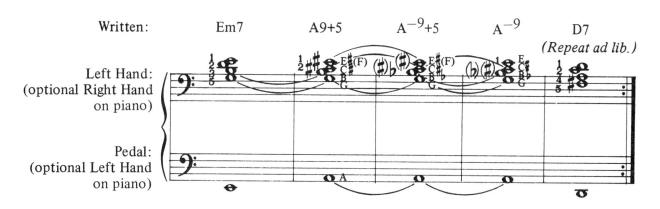

Written: Em7   A9+5   A^{-9}+5   A^{-9} D7
(Repeat ad lib.)

Left Hand:
(optional Right Hand
on piano)

Pedal:
(optional Left Hand
on piano)

Exercise 27.   Revise or find chords as necessary to play the following Progressions. (Include organ pedals. Play chords with either hand on piano):—

a)   G7^{-5} — G7 — Cmaj9 — C6
b)   Cm7^{-5} — F7 — B♭maj7 — B♭6
c)   Gm7 (High) — C9+5 — Fmaj7 — F6
d)   D7^{-5} — D7 — G7^{-5} — G7
e)   Dm7 — G^{-9}+5 — Cm7^{-5} — F7 — B♭maj7

(Answers on page 100)

SECTION TWENTY TWO   ADDED NOTES (4)
The "11th"

From the point of view of note names the "11th" of the scale is the same as the "4th" of the scale:—

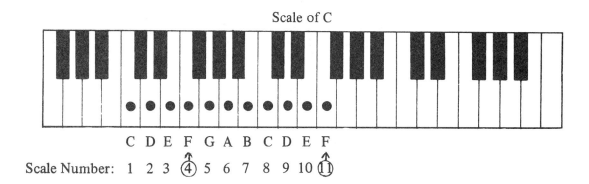

Scale of C

C D E F G A B C D E F

Scale Number: 1 2 3 ④ 5 6 7 8 9 10 ⑪

The chords "Csus4" and "C11" must therefore have at least one thing in common: the note "F".

The two chords illustrated:—

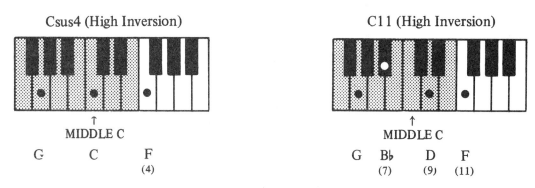

Csus4 (High Inversion)

MIDDLE C

G   C   F
(4)

C11 (High Inversion)

MIDDLE C

G B♭ D F
(7) (9) (11)

Organ pedal (piano left hand) plays "C"

The symbol "C11" is in fact short for:—

C7.9.11

and to create a true "11th" chord BOTH THE "7" AND THE "9" MUST BE PRESENT SOMEWHERE. (The Right Hand can be included here. For example the "melody" could already be playing one of the vital chord notes, such as the "7", the "9", or even the "11").

A chord such as:—

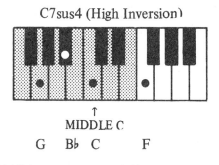

C7sus4 (High Inversion)

MIDDLE C

G B♭ C   F

is SIMILAR to "C11" but there is no "9" present, therefore its true name is "C7sus4" (C7sus)*.

*many errors occur in printed music in this area. The reader must to a certain extent use his own judgement when interpreting written chord symbols.

GENERAL METHOD FOR FINDING "11th" CHORDS

Example.   AIM: To find G11 (i.e. G7.9.11) and place it correctly (i.e. conveniently).

a)   Find the basic chord:—

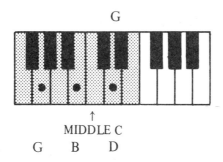

G

MIDDLE C

G   B   D

This chord is already correctly placed in the UPR.

b)   Decide which of the three notes is the "3rd":—

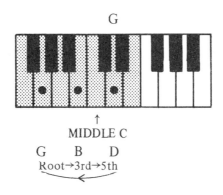

G

MIDDLE C

G   B   D

Root→3rd→5th

"B" is the 3rd.

c)   Move the 3rd up ONE half step (Major chords) or TWO half steps (Minor chords) to the 4th (same note as the 11th):—

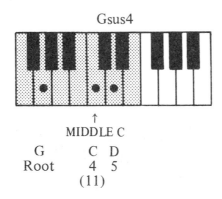

Gsus4

MIDDLE C

G   C D
Root   4 5
        (11)

69

d) Add the remaining notes required (i.e. the "7" and the "9") to turn the above chord (Gsus4) into "G11":—

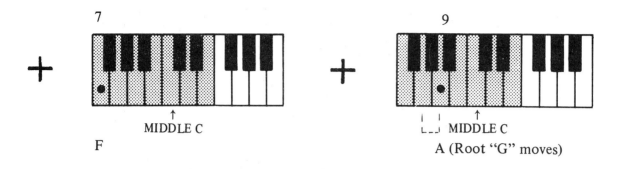

7

F

MIDDLE C

9

MIDDLE C

A (Root "G" moves)

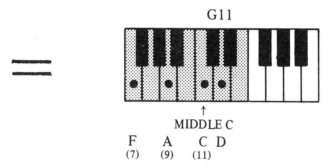

G11

MIDDLE C

F   A   C D
(7)   (9)   (11)

Organ pedal (piano left hand) plays "G" (Root)

QUICK METHOD FOR FINDING "11th" CHORDS

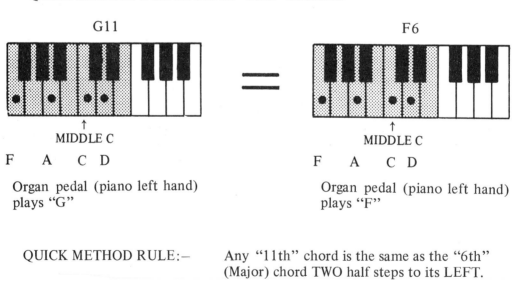

G11

MIDDLE C

F   A   C D

Organ pedal (piano left hand) plays "G"

F6

MIDDLE C

F   A   C D

Organ pedal (piano left hand) plays "F"

QUICK METHOD RULE:—   Any "11th" chord is the same as the "6th" (Major) chord TWO half steps to its LEFT.

Examples:

C11 = B♭6   A11 = G6   F11 = E♭6
   (play "C" Pedal)   (play "A" Pedal)   (play "F" Pedal)

Exercise 28.   Using either the GENERAL METHOD or the QUICK METHOD (or both) find:—

a) C11 (Normal Inversion)   d) E11
b) A11   e) F11
c) D11   f) B♭11

(Answers on page 100)

70

SECTION TWENTY THREE   THE "11th" WITH MINOR CHORDS

Although a full "Minor 11" chord is possible:—

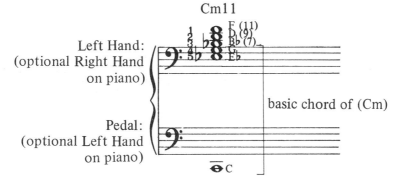

Left Hand:
(optional Right Hand
on piano)

Pedal:
(optional Left Hand
on piano)

basic chord of (Cm)

it requires a very large hand to play it, or the chord must be divided between the two hands.

Any attempts to "Invert" the above chord will lead to dissonance and "cluttering".

When Cm11 is required using one hand only it is easier to play "C11" (i.e. the MAJOR "11") and let the surrounding chords (especially the one that follows) supply the "Minor" tonality:—

Cm11 (i.e. C11) (High Inversion)   Cm7

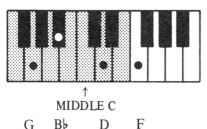   going to: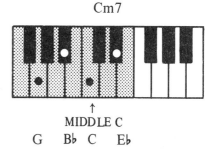

MIDDLE C   MIDDLE C

G   B♭   D   F   G   B♭   C   E♭

Organ pedal (piano left hand) plays "C"

QUICK METHOD FOR MINOR "11's" USING LEFT HAND ONLY:—

Examples: Cm11 = C11 = B♭6*
                              (play "C" Pedal)

                   Gm11 = G11 = F6
                              (play "G" Pedal)

                   Am11 = A11 = G6
                              (play "A" Pedal)

                   (and so on)

Exercise 29.   Having revised or worked out chords as necessary, play the following Progressions (with pedals, etc.):—

    a)   D11 – D9 – Dm7 – G⁻9 – Cmaj7
    b)   Am11 – Am7 – Dm9 – G⁻9 – C6
    c)   Gm11 – Gm7 – C11 (High Inversion) – C⁻9 – F6
    d)   A11 – A⁻9 – Am7 – D9 – G6
    e)   Cm11 (High Inversion) – Cm7 – F11 – F⁻9 – B♭maj7

(Answers on pages 100 and 101)

* i.e. using Quick Method Rule for "11's", Section Twenty Two, page 70.

SECTION TWENTY FOUR   ADDED NOTES (5)
The "+11" (♯11, or aug 11)

From the point of view of notes on the keyboard the "+11" is the same as the "−5":—

Scale of C

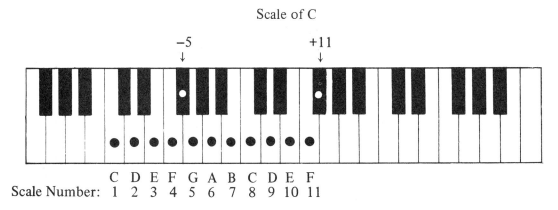

$$\begin{array}{l} -5 \ = \ G\flat \\ +11 \ = \ F\sharp \end{array} \Big\} \ \text{same note (for practical purposes)}$$

The difference in usage between the "−5" and the "+11" can be illustrated by the following two examples:—

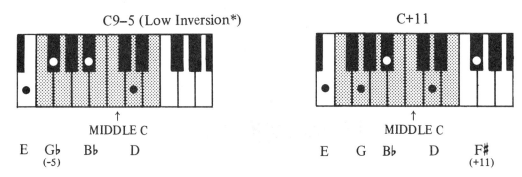

Organ pedal (piano left hand) plays "C"

In the first of the two chords above, the "5th" (G) of C9 has been flattened (flatted) to create "C9−5".

In the second of the two chords above, the "5th" (G) actually REMAINS IN THE CHORD, whilst the "+11" (F♯) is added.

Therefore:—

      C9−5 (including Root) = 5-note chord
    *C+11 (including Root) = 6-note chord

Unfortunately, for practical reasons the full six-note potential of "+11" chords cannot always be realised. For instance in the "C+11" example given above the chord is musically effective but it needs a large hand to play it. Other inversions of the chord are often not good musically and can be just as hard to play.

*for purposes of comparison

Three possible solutions for the keyboard player:—

1. Abandon the full "+11" chord and play the "9–5" chord instead (a similar chord).

    So for:—

C+11	play:	C9–5
G+11	play:	G9–5
B♭+11	play:	B♭9–5

    (and so on)

2. Play an ordinary "9" chord (e.g. C9) in the Left Hand and let the Right Hand play the "+11" note (under the melody):—

C+11 (i.e. C7.9+11)

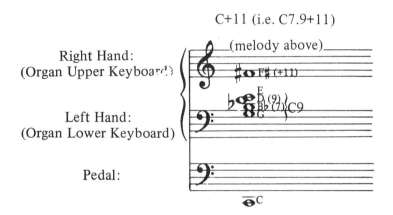

Right Hand:
(Organ Upper Keyboard)

Left Hand:
(Organ Lower Keyboard)

Pedal:

3. Play a simplified "+11" chord, omitting either the "3rd" or the "5th", or both:—

C+11 (High Inversion)

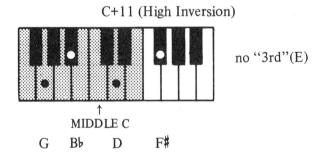

no "3rd"(E)

MIDDLE C

G   B♭   D   F♯

Organ pedal (piano left hand) plays "C"

C+11 (Normal Inversion)

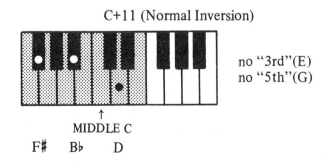

no "3rd"(E)
no "5th"(G)

MIDDLE C

F♯   B♭   D

Organ pedal (piano left hand) plays "C"

The second of the two "simplified" chords illustrated above is the same as "B♭ Augmented" (B♭+5, B♭+), that is, except for the Root Note:—

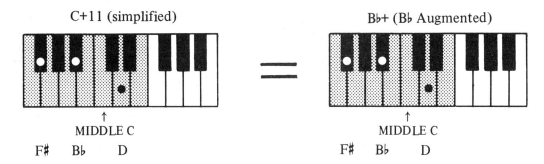

C+11 (simplified)   Bb+ (Bb Augmented)

MIDDLE C   MIDDLE C

F♯ B♭ D   F♯ B♭ D

Organ pedal (piano left hand) plays "C" (Root)   Organ pedal (piano left hand) plays "B♭" (Root)

SIMPLIFIED "+11" RULE:

Any "+11" chord (simplified version) will be the same as the Augmented chord TWO half steps (semitones) to its LEFT.

Examples:—

> G+11 = F+ (F Augmented)
> (play "G" Pedal)
>
> A+11 = G+ (G Augmented)
> (play "A" Pedal)
>
> D+11 = C+ (C Augmented)
> (play "D" Pedal)

Exercise 30.   Using Left Hand and Pedals only on organ, and either hand on piano, play:—

    a)   C+11 (4 notes, omit 3rd. High Inversion)
    b)   C+11 (3 notes, omit 3rd and 5th. Use SIMPLI-FIED "+11" RULE)
    c)   G+11 (3 notes)
    d)   A+11 (3 notes)
    e)   D+11 (3 notes)
    f)   E+11 (3 notes)
    g)   B♭+11 (3 notes)
    h)   B♭+11 (4 notes, omit 3rd but include 5th. Normal Inversion)

(Answers on page 101)

Progression 1:—   C+11 (High Inversion) — C11 (High Inversion) — C9
   — C⁻9 — Fmaj7

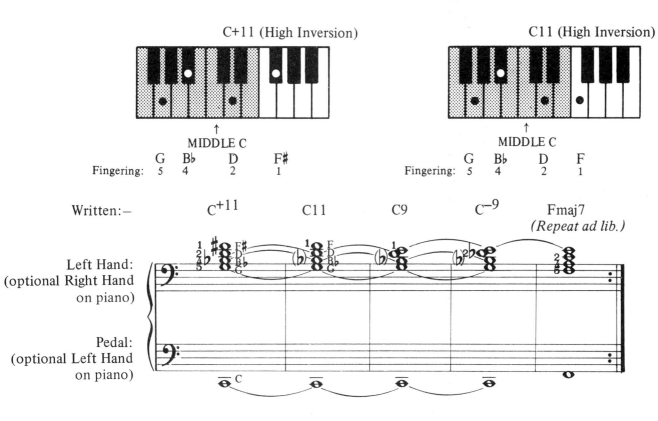

Progression 2:—   Dm9 — Dm7 — G+11 — G⁻9 — Cmaj7

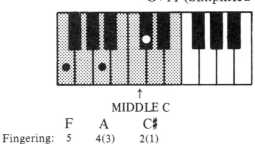

Progression 3:— Em9 (High Inversion) — Em7 — A+11 — A9

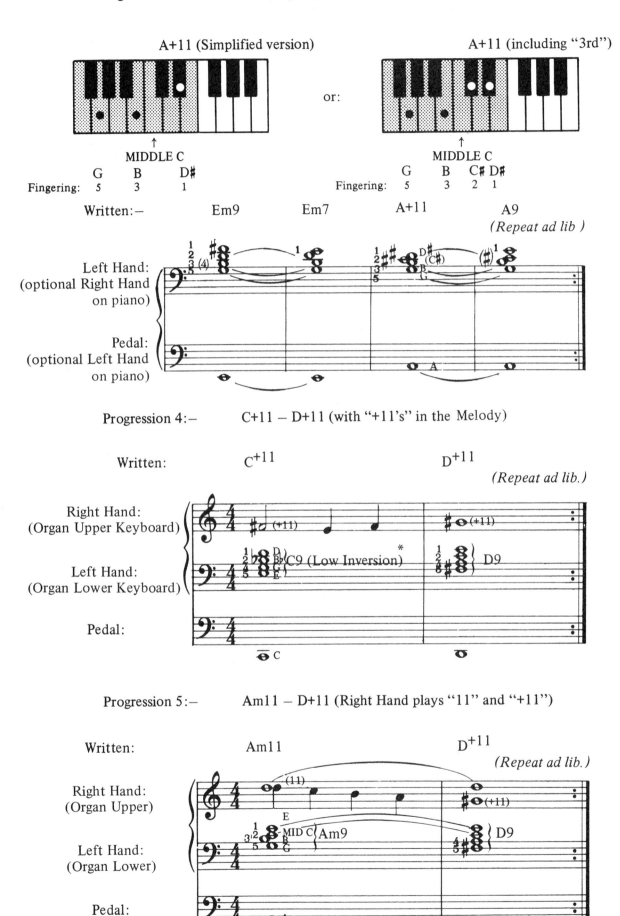

A+11 (Simplified version)   or: A+11 (including "3rd")

MIDDLE C   MIDDLE C

G   B   D♯   G   B   C♯ D♯
Fingering: 5   3   1   Fingering: 5   3   2   1

Written:—   Em9   Em7   A+11   A9
                                                (Repeat ad lib)

Left Hand:
(optional Right Hand
on piano)

Pedal:
(optional Left Hand
on piano)

Progression 4:— C+11 — D+11 (with "+11's" in the Melody)

Written: C⁺¹¹   D⁺¹¹
                                        (Repeat ad lib.)

Right Hand:
(Organ Upper Keyboard)

Left Hand:
(Organ Lower Keyboard)

Pedal:

Progression 5:— Am11 — D+11 (Right Hand plays "11" and "+11")

Written: Am11   D⁺¹¹
                                        (Repeat ad lib.)

Right Hand:
(Organ Upper)

Left Hand:
(Organ Lower)

Pedal:

*The Low Inversion of C9 sounds best here because all the notes are nicely separated. It also matches the "shape" of the next chord (D9), which is convenient.

76

Exercise 31. Find the following "9" chords for Left Hand and Pedals
(organ), and either hand (piano):—

  a) Db9
  b) Eb9 (High Inversion)
  c) E9 (High Inversion)

Using both hands on piano, and Right Hand in addition to
Left Hand and Pedals on organ, play:—

  d) Db+11
  e) Eb+11 (Left Hand High)
  f) E+11 (Left Hand High)

Using Left Hand and Pedals only on organ, and either hand
on piano, play the following Progression:—

  g) C9 (Low Inversion) — Db9 — D9 — Eb9 (High Inver-
      sion) — E9 (High Inversion)

Using both hands on piano, and both hands and pedals on
organ, play the following Progression:—

  h) C+11 (Left Hand Low) — Db+11 — D+11 — Eb+11
      (Left Hand High — E+11 (Left Hand High)

      (Answers on page 101)

ADDED NOTES (6)
The "13th"

From the point of view of note names the "13th" of the scale is the same as the "6th" of the scale:—

Scale of C

C D E F G A B C D E F G A

Scale number: 1 2 3 4 5 ⑥ 7 8 9 10 11 12 ⑬

The difference in the treatment of the two notes can be illustrated by the following:—

$$C6 = C + 6$$
$$C13 = C + 7 + 6 \text{ (i.e. 13)}$$

In other words a "13th" chord must include BOTH A "7" AND A "6" (13) IN IT SOMEWHERE.

GENERAL METHOD FOR "13's" (Left Hand only on organ, either hand on piano)

1. Find appropriate "7" chord (4 notes), placing it correctly in the UPR.

2. Decide which of the notes is the "5th".

3. Move 5th UP TWO HALF STEPS to the "6" (13).

4. Omit Root.

Example 1.   AIM:— To find "C13" and place it correctly.

1.

C7

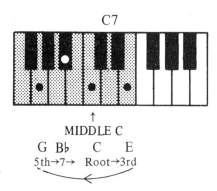

correctly placed in the UPR

↑
MIDDLE C
G Bb   C   E
5th→7→ Root→3rd

2.   The 5th is "G"

3.   Move 5th up two half steps to the "6" (13):—

C13

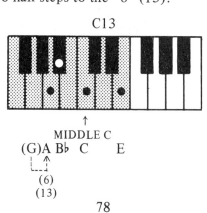

↑
MIDDLE C
(G)A Bb C   E

(6)
(13)

4. Omit Root.

C13

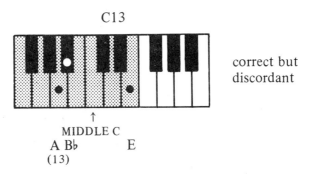

correct but
discordant

MIDDLE C
A B♭   E
(13)

Organ pedal (piano left hand) plays "C" (Root)

The "tension" in the above chord can be relieved considerably by Inverting
the chord upwards:—

C13 (High Inversion)

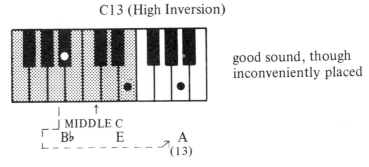

good sound, though
inconveniently placed

MIDDLE C
B♭   E   A
(13)

Organ pedal (piano left hand) plays "C" (Root)

Which of the above two Inversions of "C13" you use depends on musical
context and technical considerations.

ALTERNATIVE METHOD FOR "13's" (Using Both Hands)

Using "C13" as an example:—

1. Left Hand plays "C7"

2. Right Hand plays note "A" (i.e. the "13" (6)) under the Melody:—

Right Hand:
(Organ Upper Keyboard)

Left Hand:
(Organ Lower Keyboard)

Pedal:

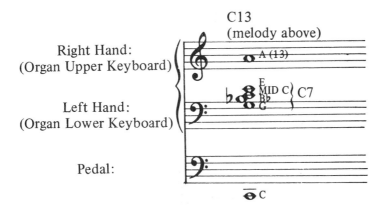

C13
(melody above)

A (13)

E
MID C } C7
B♭
C

C

79

Example 2.   AIM:— To find "G13" and place it correctly.

1.

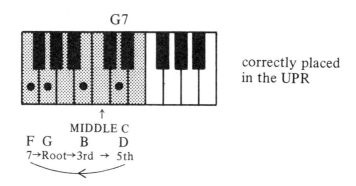

G7

correctly placed in the UPR

↑
MIDDLE C
F   G   B   D
7→Root→3rd → 5th

2.   The 5th is "D"

3.   Move the 5th UP two half steps to the "6" (13):—

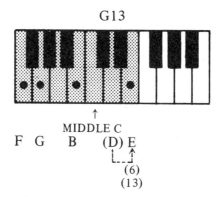

G13

↑
MIDDLE C
F   G   B   (D) E
                  └--┘↑
                   (6)
                   (13)

4.   Omit Root.

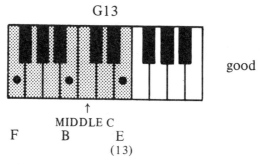

G13

good

↑
MIDDLE C
F   B   E
                   (13)

Organ pedal (piano left hand) plays "G" (Root)

Since the above chord is quite acceptable to the ear there is no need to Invert it.

Exercise 32.   Using the GENERAL METHOD given above find the following chords. (Use left hand and pedals only on organ; use either hand on piano):—

　　　　a)   A13 (High Inversion)
　　　　b)   A♭13 (High Inversion)
　　　　c)   B♭13 (High Inversion)

Using the ALTERNATIVE METHOD given above find the following two-handed chords (include pedals on organ):—

　　　　d)   D13
　　　　e)   F13
　　　　f)   E13

(Answers on page 101)

CHORD PROGRESSIONS (8)
Featuring "13's"

Progression 1:–   Dm9 – G13 – C6

G13

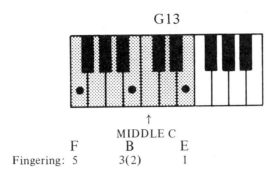

↑
MIDDLE C
F   B   E
Fingering: 5   3(2)   1

Written:–   Dm9   G13   C6
                                          (Repeat ad lib.)

Left Hand:
(optional Right Hand
on piano)

Pedal:
(optional Left Hand
on piano)

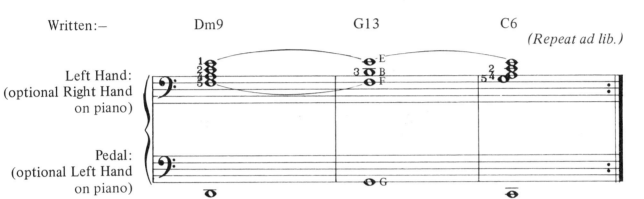

Progression 2:–   A13 (High Inversion) – D9 – G13 – G⁻9 – Cmaj7

A13 (High Inversion)

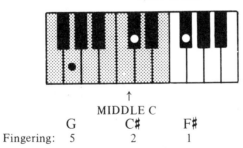

↑
MIDDLE C
G   C♯   F♯
Fingering: 5   2   1

Written:–   A13   D9   G13   G⁻9   Cmaj7
                                       (Repeat ad lib.)

Left Hand:
(optional Right Hand
on piano)

Pedal:
(optional Left Hand
on piano)

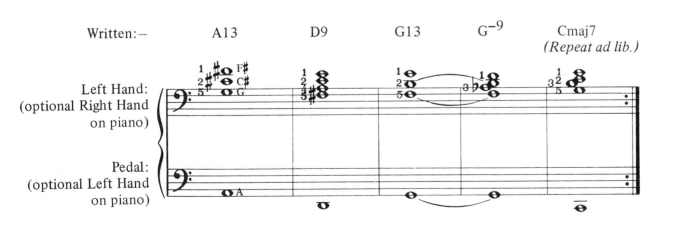

Progression 3:— D13 – G13 – Gm9 – C13 – Fmaj7 (Using both hands as required)

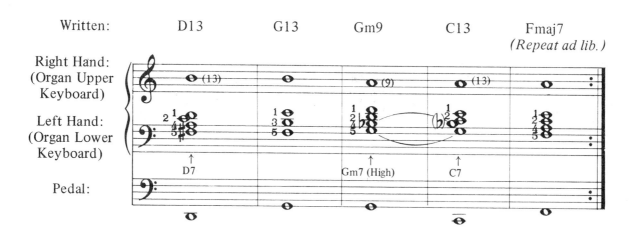

Exercise 33.   Using either hand on piano, and Left Hand and Pedals only on organ, play the following Progressions:—

a) Gm7 (High Inversion) – C13 (High Inversion) – Fmaj7 – F#°

b) A13 (High Inversion) – A7 – A7^{-5} – A7 (Omit "Root" from chord throughout)

c) B♭13 (High Inversion) – A13 (High Inversion) – A♭13 (High Inversion) – G13

Play appropriate Left Hand chords (and pedals on organ) under the following melodic fragments:—

(Answers on page 102)

From the point of view of notes on the keyboard the "–13" is the same as the "+5":—

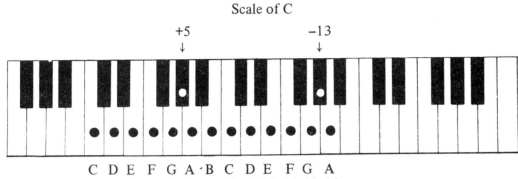

Scale of C

C	D	E	F	G	A	B	C	D	E	F	G	A

Scale number: 1 2 3 4 5 6 7 8 9 10 11 12 13

$$-13 = A♭$$
$$+5 = G♯$$ same note (for practical purposes)

However, these two apparently identical notes give rise to different Chord Symbols:—

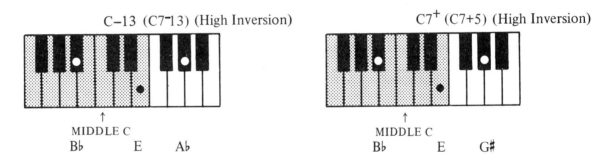

C–13 (C7⁻13) (High Inversion)   C7⁺ (C7+5) (High Inversion)

MIDDLE C   MIDDLE C
B♭   E   A♭   B♭   E   G♯

Organ pedal (piano left hand) plays "C"

GENERAL METHOD FOR "–13's" (one hand only)

1. Find appropriate "7" chord (4 notes), placing it correctly in the UPR.

2. Decide which of the notes is the "5th".

3. Move 5th up ONE half step to the "–13" (in doing so give it a new LETTER name, e.g. if 5th is "D", the "–13" will be called "E♭", not "D♯")

4. Omit Root.

Example:—   AIM:— To find "G–13", place it correctly, and name the notes correctly.

1.

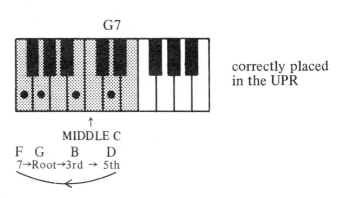

G7

correctly placed in the UPR

↑
MIDDLE C

F   G   B   D
7→Root→3rd → 5th

2.   The 5th is "D"

3.   Move 5th up ONE half step to the "–13":—

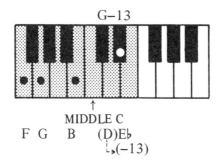

G–13

↑
MIDDLE C

F   G   B   (D)E♭
⌐,(–13)

The "–13" is "E♭". ("D♯" would be the "+5" and would therefore be an incorrect NAME for the note).

4.   Omit Root.

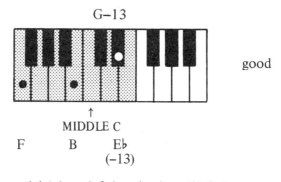

G–13

good

↑
MIDDLE C

F   B   E♭
(–13)

Organ pedal (piano left hand) plays "G" (Root)

Since the above chord is quite acceptable to the ear there is no need to Invert it or divide it between the hands. BUT EITHER OF THESE ALTERNATIVES IS AVAILABLE IF NECESSARY OR DESIRED, e.g.:—

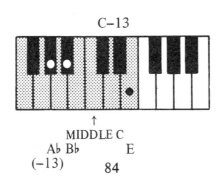

C–13

↑
MIDDLE C

A♭ B♭   E
(–13)

84

could be played like this:—

C–13 (High Inversion)

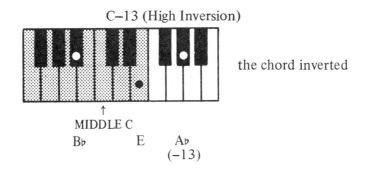

the chord inverted

↑
MIDDLE C
B♭   E   A♭
                (–13)

or like this:—

C⁻¹³
(melody above)

Right Hand:
(Organ Upper Keyboard)

Left Hand:
(Organ Lower Keyboard)

Pedal:

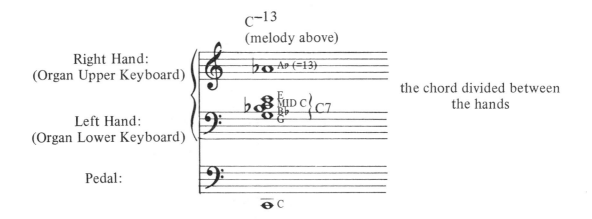

the chord divided between
the hands

Exercise 34.   Using the GENERAL METHOD given above, find the following chords. (Use only left hand and pedals on organ; use
either hand on piano. Be careful to name the notes correctly):—

    a)   A–13 (High Inversion)
    b)   A♭–13
    c)   B♭–13 (High Inversion)
    d)   B–13 (High Inversion)

By raising the appropriate note of "B–13" by one half step,
play:—

    e)   B13 (High Inversion)

Using Both Hands (and pedals on organ) play:—

    f)   D–13
    g)   F–13
    h)   E–13

(Answers on page 102)

CHORD PROGRESSIONS (9)
Featuring "–13's"

Progression 1:–   G13 – G⁻13 – G11 – G⁻9 – C6

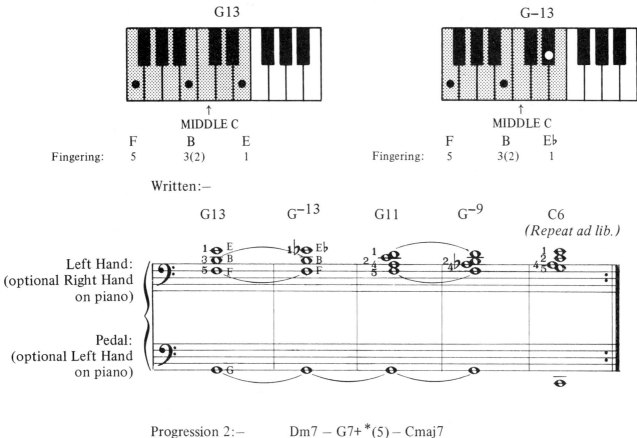

Progression 2:–   Dm7 – G7+*(5) – Cmaj7

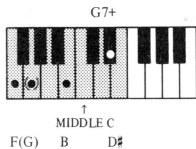

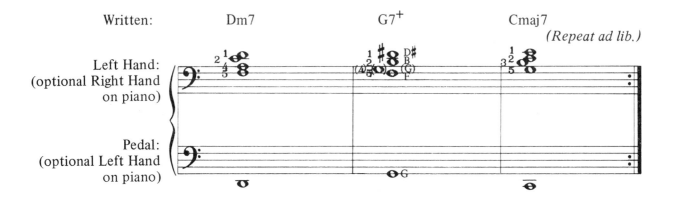

*In a "rising" Progression such as this the chord would probably be written this way rather than "G–13".

Progression 3:— A13 (High Inversion) — A⁻13 (High Inversion) — Ab13 (High Inversion) — Ab⁻13 — G6

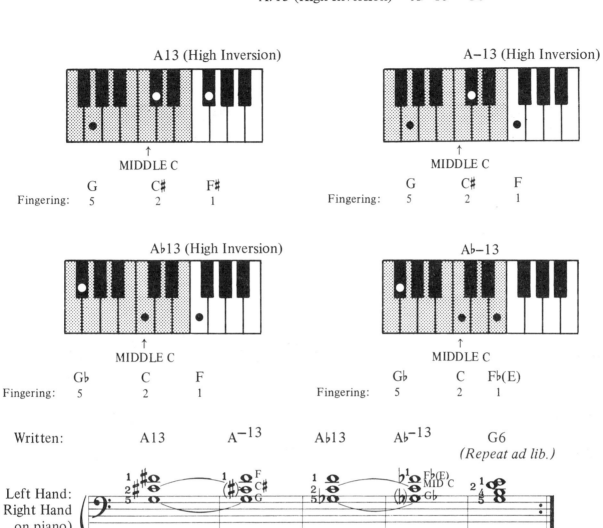

Written: A13   A⁻13   Ab13   Ab⁻13   G6
(Repeat ad lib.)

Left Hand:
(optional Right Hand
on piano)

Pedal:
(optional Left Hand
on piano)

Progression 4:— D13 — D⁻13 — C13 — C⁻13 — Fmaj9 (Using both hands throughout).

Written: D13   D⁻13   C13   C⁻13   Fmaj9
(Repeat ad lib.)

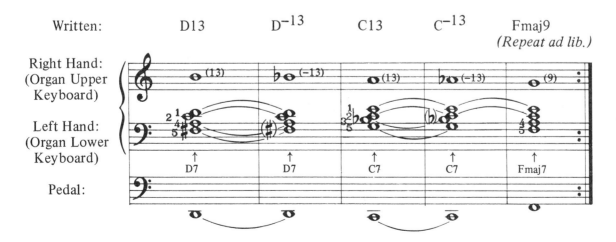

Right Hand:
(Organ Upper
Keyboard)

Left Hand:
(Organ Lower
Keyboard)

Pedal:

Exercise 35. Using either hand on piano, and left hand and pedals only on organ, play the following Progressions:—

a) G13 – G⁻13 – Dm7 – G7+ – Cmaj7
b) B♭13 (High Inversion) – B♭⁻13 (High Inversion) – A13 (High Inversion) – A⁻13 (High Inversion) – Dm6.9
c) A7⁻5 – A7 – A7+ – A13 – A⁻13 – A7 (Omit "Root" from chord throughout)

Play appropriate Left Hand chords (and pedals on organ) under the following melodic fragments:—

d)

(Answers on pages 102 and 103)

The following "Staircase" illustrates the various "Added Notes" described in this book:—

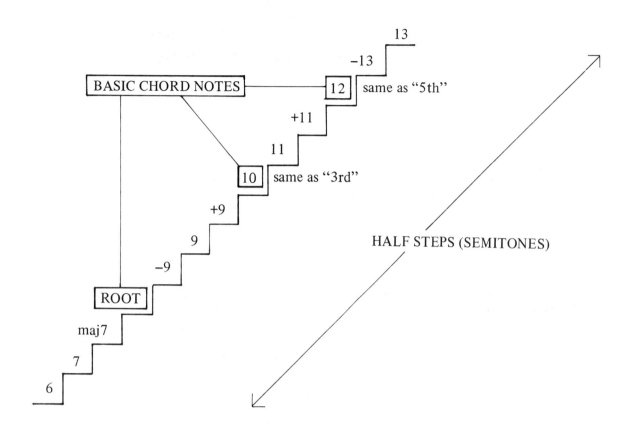

A large number of Added Note "mixtures" are theoretically possible, but many of them have little or no musical value or are not playable by the average size hand(s).

The mixtures that are available are used mainly with Major chords, though the occasional Minor chord mixture is possible.

Here is a list of the mixtures already dealt with in this book (using the chord of "C" as an example):—

C6.9	Cmaj9		SECTION ELEVEN
Cm6.9	Cm(maj9)		
C–9	C9	C+9	SECTIONS ELEVEN AND TWELVE
——*	Cm9	——*	
C11	C+11		SECTIONS TWENTY TWO, TWENTY
Cm11	——*		THREE, AND TWENTY FOUR
C13	C–13		SECTIONS TWENTY SIX AND
——*	——*		TWENTY EIGHT

* The corresponding Minor chord unsatisfactory, or rare

Here next is a list of useful mixtures not yet dealt with (Minor equivalents unsatisfactory, or rare):—

C13.9   C13–9   C–13.9*   C–13–9
C13.11(9)   C13.11–9   C13+11(9)

All the above mixtures include the "7", which can be included in the Chord Symbol, e.g.:—

C7.13.9, C7.13–9 (etc.)

Applying the above mixtures to Chord Progressions (using basic chord "G"):—

Progression 1:—   G13.9 – G13⁻9 – C6

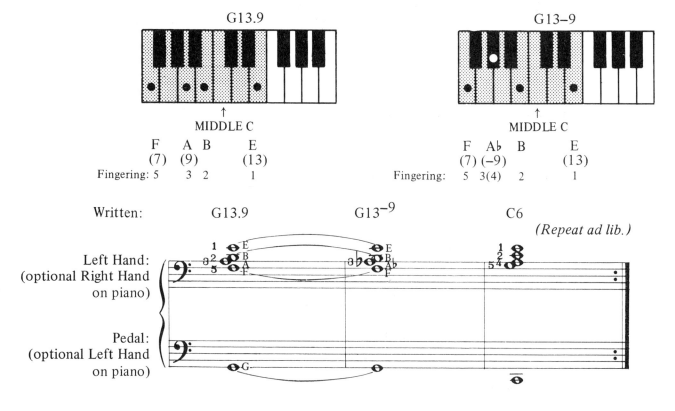

Written: G13.9   G13⁻9   C6

Progression 2:—   G13.11.9 – G13.11⁻9 – G13⁻9 – G⁻13⁻9 – C6

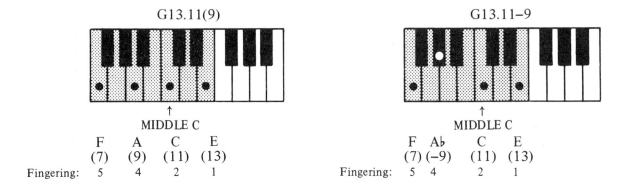

* could be written: C9+5 (same chord in practice)

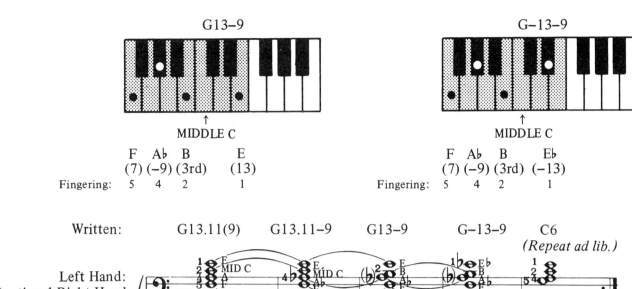

G13–9

MIDDLE C

F	Ab	B	E
(7)	(–9)	(3rd)	(13)
Fingering:			
5	4	2	1

G–13–9

MIDDLE C

F	Ab	B	Eb
(7)	(–9)	(3rd)	(–13)
Fingering:			
5	4	2	1

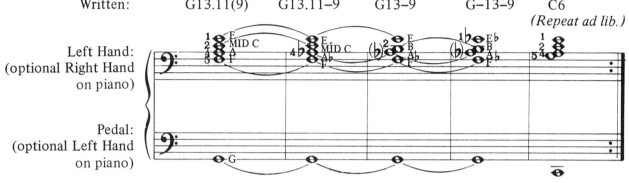

Written: G13.11(9)   G13.11–9   G13–9   G–13–9   C6
(Repeat ad lib.)

Left Hand:
(optional Right Hand
on piano)

Pedal:
(optional Left Hand
on piano)

Progression 3:–   G13+11(9) – G9 – Cmaj9

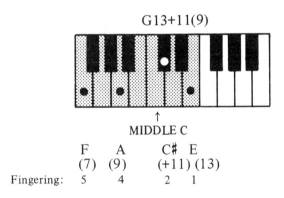

G13+11(9)

MIDDLE C

F	A	C♯	E
(7)	(9)	(+11)	(13)
Fingering:			
5	4	2	1

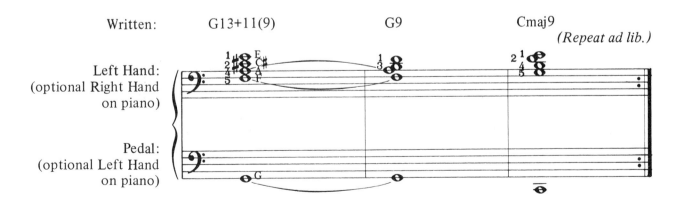

Written: G13+11(9)   G9   Cmaj9
(Repeat ad lib.)

Left Hand:
(optional Right Hand
on piano)

Pedal:
(optional Left Hand
on piano)

91

Exercise 36.   Using either hand on piano, left hand and pedals only on organ, play the following Progressions:—

a)   A13+11(9) (High Inversion) — A9 — D9 — G13.9 — Cmaj9

b)   A13.9 (High Inversion) — A⁻13.9 (High Inversion) — D9 — G13⁻9 — Cmaj9

c)   A13.11(9) (High Inversion) — A⁻13⁻9 (High Inversion) — Am7 — A♭13.9 (High Inversion) — Gmaj9

Play appropriate Left Hand Chords (and pedals on organ) under the following melodic fragments:—

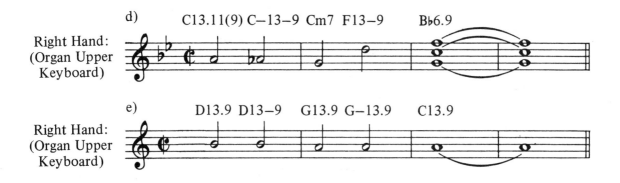

d)   C13.11(9) C—13—9 Cm7 F13—9   B♭6.9

Right Hand:
(Organ Upper
Keyboard)

e)   D13.9 D13—9   G13.9 G—13.9   C13.9

Right Hand:
(Organ Upper
Keyboard)

(Answers on page 103)

SECTION THIRTY ONE   CHORD MIXTURES WITH "+5" AND "–5"

Occasionally a chord mixture such as C+9* (i.e. C7+9) has its "5th" sharpened (sharped) or flattened (flatted). In this case the chord symbol would read:—

C+9+5 (or C7+9+5)
C+9–5 (or C7+9–5)

Often both hands are needed to "voice" such chords effectively:—

Progression 1:—   C+9+5 – C+9⁻5 – Fmaj9

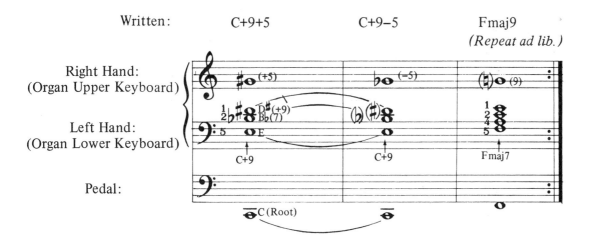

Progression 2:—   C13 – C⁻13⁻5 – Fmaj9

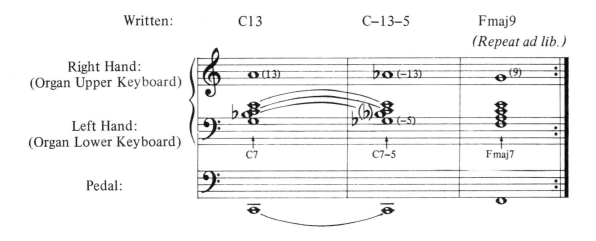

*for a review of this chord refer to SECTION TWELVE, page 35.

Exercise 37. Play appropriate Left Hand Chords (and pedals on organ)
under the following melodic fragments:—

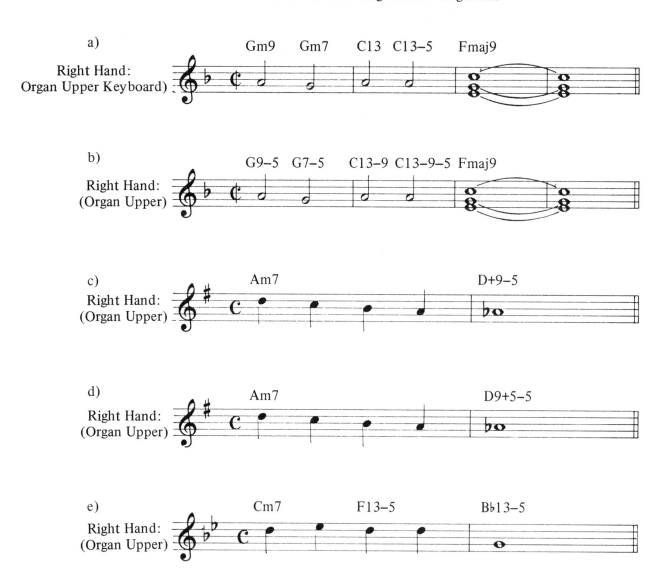

(Answers on page 103)

The Answers give the correct NOTE NAMES as they would appear on the keyboard from LEFT TO RIGHT in the "Middle C" area (approximate).

Actual "Middle C's" appear in "boxes" as an aid to correct location on the keyboard.

Exercise 1.

a) Bb Db F
b) [C] Eb Gb
c) Bb D F#
d) G B D
e) G Bb D
f) F Ab Cb(B)
g) D F# A
h) F A [C]
i) F Ab [C]
j) G Bb Db
k) G B D#
l) F A C#

(handwritten: 29|4|20)
(handwritten: 12/12)

Exercise 2.

a) G B D
b) G# B E
c) G Bb Eb
d) G Bb D
e) F A D
f) G Bb Db
g) F B D
h) G C# E
i) G B D#
j) F# A# D

(handwritten: 8/10)

Exercise 3.

a) G B D
b) F# A D
c) F A [C]
d) G# B E
e) A C# E

(handwritten: 4/5)

Exercise 4.

a) F G B D
b) F# A [C] D
c) F A [C] Eb
d) G# B D E
e) G A C# E
f) G B D E
g) F A [C] D
h) F A [C] E

(handwritten: 8/8)

Exercise 5.

a) G [C] Eb
b) G Bb D
c) F A D
d) F Ab [C]
e) G B E
f) A [C] E

Exercise 6.

a) G A [C] Eb
b) F G Bb D
c) F A [C] D
d) F Ab [C] D
e) G B D E
f) G A [C] E
g) G B [C] Eb
h) F A [C] E

Exercise 7.

a) F# A [C] D – F G B D – F# A [C] D
(pedal/piano left hand: D)   (pedal: G)   (pedal: D)

b) G A C# E – F# A [C] D – G A C# E
(ped: A)   (ped: D)   (ped: A)

c) G A [C] E – G A C# E – F# A [C] D –
(ped: C)   (ped: A)   (ped: D)

F G B D – G A [C] E
(ped: G)   (ped: C)

d) G B [C] E – G A [C] E – F A [C] D –
(ped: C ——————————————)   (ped: F)

F G B D – G A [C] E
(ped: G)   (ped: C)

e) G B [C] E   – G A [C] E   – F A [C] D   –
   (ped: C)   (ped: A)   (ped: D)

   F G B D   – G A [C] E
   (ped: G)   (ped: C)

f) G B [C] E   – F A [C] E   – G B [C] E
   (ped: C)   (ped: F)   (ped: C)

g) G B [C] E   – F A [C] E   – F A [C] D   –
   (ped: C)   (ped: F)   (ped: D)

   F G B D   – G A [C] E
   (ped: G)   (ped: C)

Exercise 8.

a) G   B♭ D   F ⎫
b) G   B♭ D   F♯ ⎬ (ped: G)
c) E   G♯ B   D♯   (ped: E)
d) E♭ G   B♭ D   (ped: E♭)

Exercise 10.

a) F   A♭ B   D   (ped: B)
b) G   B♭ D♭ E   (ped: G)
c) F   A♭ B   D   (ped: D)
d) F♯ A   [C] E♭ (ped: A)
e) G♭ A   [C] E♭ (ped: E♭)

Exercise 9.

a) G   B♭ C♯   E   (ped: C♯)
b) G   B♭ D♭(C♯) F♭(E) (ped: B♭)
    a) and b) are the same except
    for:
    1. the Pedal note
    2. the NAMING of the notes
        (unimportant in the case
        of Diminished chords)

c) F   A♭ C♭(B) D (ped: F)
d) F   G   B   D♯   (ped: G)
e) F   A   C♯ E♭   (ped: F)

Exercise 11.

a) G [C] E – G♯ [C] E – F A [C] D – F A♭ [C] D – G A [C] E
   (ped: C ——————)   (ped: F ——————————————)   (ped: C)

b) G A [C] E – G A C♯ E – F A [C] D – F G B D♯ – G A [C] E
   (ped: C)   (ped: A)   (ped: D)   (ped: G)   (ped: C)

c) F A [C] – F A C♯ – F B♭ D
   (ped: F——————)   (ped: B♭)

d) F A [C] – F A C♯ – F B♭ D – F G B D♯ – G A [C] E
   (ped: F——————)   (ped: B♭)   (ped: G)   (ped: C)

e) G A [C] E – G B♭ C♯ E – F A [C] D – F G B D♯ – G A [C] E
   (ped: C)   (ped: C♯)   (ped: D)   (ped: G)   (ped: C)

96

Exercise 12.

a) E
b) E♭
c) E♯(F)
d) E♭♭(D)
e) E
f) E♭
g) A♯
h) A
i) A♭

Exercise 13.

a) G A [C] ⎱ (ped: F)
b) G A♭ [C] ⎰
c) G D E♭ (ped: C)
d) G♯ B F♯ ⎱ (ped: E)
e) G B F♯ ⎰

Exercise 14.

a) F G [C] D ⎱
b) F A♭ [C] D ⎬ (ped: B♭)
c) F A [C] D ⎰
d) F A B D ⎱
e) F♯ A B D ⎬ (ped: G)
f) A B D E ⎰

Exercise 15.

a) F A B D ⎱
b) F A B E ⎮
c) F A [C] D ⎬ (ped: D)
d) F A [C] E ⎮
e) F A C♯ D ⎮
f) F A C♯ E ⎰

g) G B C♯ E ⎱
h) G B C♯ F♯ ⎮
i) G B D E ⎬ (ped: E)
j) G B D F♯ ⎮
k) G B D♯ (E) ⎮
l) G B D♯ F♯ ⎰

Exercise 16.

a) F A♭ C♭(B) D (ped: B♭)
b) F A♭ B D (ped: G)
c) The Pedal notes are different. The "naming" of one of the notes (C♭) is different. For practical purposes the chords are the same except for the Pedals.
d) F♯ A [C] E♭ (ped: D)
e) G B♭ C♯ E (ped: A)

Exercise 17.

a) F♯ A [C] E♯(F) ⎱ (ped: D)
b) F♯ [C] E♯(F) ⎰
c) F A♭ C♭(B) D♭ ⎱
d) F A♭ C♭(B) E ⎬ (ped: D♭)
e) F C♭(B) E ⎰
f) G B♭ D♭ E♭ ⎱
g) G B♭ D♭ F♯ ⎬ (ped: E♭)
h) G D♭ F♯ ⎰

Exercise 18.

a) F A [C] E – F♯ A [C] E♭ – F A [C] D – F G B D – G A [C] E
   (ped: F)   (ped: D ——————————————————)   (ped: G)   (ped: C)

b) F A [C] D – F A♭ B D – G A [C] E
   (ped: D)   (ped: G)   (ped: C)

c) F A [C] D – F A♭ B D – G B [C] E – G A [C] E
   (ped: D)   (ped: G)   (ped: C ————————————)

d) F A [C] E – F♯ A [C] E♭ – F A [C] D – F A♭ B D – G B [C] E –
   (ped: F)   (ped: D ——————————————————)   (ped: G)   (ped: C ——————

   G A [C] E
   ——————————)

97

e) F G B♭ D – E B♭ D♯ – F A [C] E – F A [C] D
    (ped: G)   (ped: C)   (ped: F ————————————————)

f) G A [C] E – F♯ [C] E♯(F) – F G B♭ D – E B♭ D♯ – F A [C] E
    (ped: A)   (ped: D)   (ped: G)   (ped: C)   (ped: F)

g) G B [C] E – G A [C] E – F♯ [C] E♯(F) – F A♭ B D – G A [C] E
    (ped: C)   (ped: A)   (ped: D)   (ped: G)   (ped: C)

Exercise 19.

a) G B D E – G A [C] E – F A [C] D – F G B D – G A [C] E
    (ped: C)   (ped: A)   (ped: D)   (ped: G)   (ped: C)

b) G A D E – G A C♯ E – F A [C] D – F G B D – G A [C] E
    (ped: C)   (ped: A)   (ped: D)   (ped: G)   (ped: C)

c) G A [C] E – G B♭ D E – F A [C] D – F A♭ [C] D – G A [C] E
    (ped: C ——————————————————————)   (ped: F ——————————————————————)   (ped: C)

d) G D E – G [C] E – F A [C] E – F A♭ [C] D – G B [C] E
    (ped: C ————————————————)   (ped: F ————————————————————)   (ped: C)

e) G D E♭ – G [C] E♭ – F♯ A [C] D – F A♭ B D – G A [C] E♭
    (ped: C ————————————————)   (ped: D)   (ped: G)   (ped: C)

f) G B D E – G A [C] E – F A B D – F A♭ B D – G A [C] E
    (ped: C ————————————————————————)   (ped: G ————————————————————)   (ped: C)

g) G B D E – G A [C] E – F A [C] E – F A♭ B D – G A [C] E
    (ped: C)   (ped: A)   (ped: D)   (ped: G)   (ped: C)

h) G B D E – G B♭ C♯ E – F♯ A [C] E – F A♭ B D – G B [C] E
    (ped: C)   (ped: A)   (ped: D)   (ped: G)   (ped: C)

Exercise 20.

a) F B♭ [C]   (ped: F)
b) A D E   (ped: A)
c) G A D   (ped: D)
d) A B E   (ped: E)
e) A♭ B♭ E♭   (ped: E♭)

Exercise 21.

a) F B♭ E♭ – F B♭ D – G [C] D – G B D – G [C] E
    (ped: B♭ ————————————————)   (ped: G ————————————————)   (ped: C)

b) G [C] F – F B♭ E♭ – G [C] D – G B D – G [C] E
    (ped: C)   (ped: B♭)   (ped: G ————————————————)   (ped: C)

c) F Bb [C] – F A [C] – G [C] D – G B D – A D E – A C# E
(ped: F ————————————)   (ped: G————————)   (ped: A ——————————)

d) F Bb Eb – F Bb D – G [C] F – G [C] E – G A D – F# A D
(ped: Bb ————————————)   (ped: C————————)   (ped: D ——————————)

e) F Bb [C] – F A [C] – Ab Bb Eb – G Bb Eb – G A D
(ped: F ————————————)   (ped: Eb ——————————)   (ped: D)

Exercise 22.

a) G [C] F – G [C] Eb – F Ab [C] D – F G B D – G A [C] Eb
(ped: C ————————————)   (ped: F)   (ped: G)   (ped: C)

b) G [C] D – G Bb D – F Bb [C] – F Ab [C] – G [C] D – G B D
(ped: G ————————————)   (ped: F——————————)   (ped: G ——————————)

c) A D E – A [C] E – G [C] D – G Bb D – A C# E
(ped: A ——————————)   (ped: G ——————————)   (ped: A)

d) A D E – A [C] E – A D E – A C# E – G A D – F# A D
(ped: A ———————————————————————————)   (ped: D ——————————)

e) G [C] F – G [C] Eb – G [C] D – G Bb D – A D E*
(ped: C ————————————)   (ped: G——————————)   (ped: A)

*Although this "sus 4" chord does not resolve here, its title implies that some sort of "A Major" chord would follow.

Exercise 23.

a) F G [C] D }
b) F G [C] D }   (ped: G)
c) G A [C] D   (ped: D)
d) F Bb [C] Eb   (ped: F)
e) G A D E   (ped: A)

Exercise 24.

a) G A [C] E – G A [C] E – F G [C] D – F G B D – G A [C] E
(ped: C)   (ped: A)   (ped: G ——————————————————————)   (ped: C)

b) G A [C] D – F# A [C] D – F G [C] D – F G B D – G B [C] E
(ped: D ————————————————)   (ped: G ——————————————)   (ped: C)

c) F G [C] D – F G Bb D – G Bb [C] F – G Bb [C] E – F A [C] E
(ped: G ————————————————)   (ped: C ——————————————)   (ped: F)

d) G A D E – G A [C] E – G A [C] D – F Ab B D – G A [C] E
(ped: A ————————————————)   (ped: D)   (ped: G)   (ped: C)

99

e) G A D E – G A C♯ E – G A [C] D – F♯ A [C] D – G B D E
(ped: A ————————————————————) (ped: D ————————————) (ped: G)

Exercise 25.

a) F♯ A♯ D ⎫
b) F♯ A♭ D ⎭ (ped: D)

c) A C♯ E♯(F) ⎫
d) A C♯ E♭ ⎭ (ped: A)

e) G♯ [C] E♭ ⎫
f) G♭ [C] E♭ ⎭ (ped: C)

g) G B♭ D♯ ⎫
h) G B♭ D♭ ⎭ (ped: G)

i) F A♯ D ⎫
j) F A♭ D ⎭ (ped: D)

k) A [C] E♯(F) ⎫
l) A [C] E♭ ⎭ (ped: A)

Exercise 26.

a) F G B♭ D♭ ⎫
b) G B♭ D♭ F ⎬ (ped: G)
c) F G B D♭ ⎭

d) F♯ A♭ [C] D (ped: D)
e) G A [C] E♭ (ped: A)
f) F A B D♯ (ped: B)

g) F♯ A♯ [C] E (ped: D)

h) G B C♯ E♯(F) ⎫
i) G B♭ C♯ E♯(F) ⎭ (ped: A)

j) F A♭ B D♯ (ped: G)
k) G♭ A C♭(B) E♭ (ped: F)
l) F G♯ B♭ D (ped: E)

Exercise 27.

a) F G B D♭ – F G B D – G B D E – G A [C] E
(ped: G ————————————————) (ped: C ————————————————)

b) G♭ B♭ [C] E♭ – F A [C] E♭ – F A B♭ D – F G B♭ D
(ped: C)   (ped: F)   (ped: B♭ ————————————————)

c) G B♭ D F – G♯ B♭ D E – F A [C] E – F A [C] D
(ped: G)   (ped: C)   (ped: F ————————————————)

d) F♯ A♭ [C] D – F♯ A [C] D – F G B D♭ – F G B D
(ped: D ————————————————) (ped: G ————————————————)

e) F A [C] D – F A♭ B D♯ – G♭ B♭ [C] E♭ – F A [C] E♭ – F A B♭ D
(ped: D)   (ped: G)   (ped: C)   (ped: F)   (ped: B♭)

Exercise 28.

a) F G B♭ D (ped: C)
b) G B D E (ped: A)
c) G A [C] E (ped: D)
d) F♯ A B D (ped: E)
e) G B♭ [C] E♭ (ped: F)
f) F A♭ [C] E♭ (ped: B♭)

Exercise 29.

a) G A [C] E – F♯ A [C] E – F A [C] D – F A♭ B D – G B [C] E
(ped: D ————————————————————————) (ped: G)   (ped: C)

100

b)   G   B   D   E   –G   A   [C]   E   –F   A   [C]   E   –F   A♭   B   D   –G   A   [C]   E
    (ped: A ——————————————————————)   (ped: D)   (ped: G)   (ped: C)

c)   F   A   [C]   D   –F   G   B♭   D   –G   B♭   D   F   –G   B♭   D♭   E   –F   A   [C]   D
    (ped: G ——————————————————————)   (ped: C ———————————————————)   (ped: F)

d)   G   B   D   E   –G   B♭   C♯   E   –G   A   [C]   E   –F♯   A   [C]   E   –G   B   D   E
    (ped: A ——————————————————————————————)   (ped: D)   (ped: G)

e)   G   B♭   D   F   –G   B♭   [C]   E♭   –G   B♭   [C]   E♭   –G♭   A   [C]   E♭   –F   A   B♭   D
    (ped: C ——————————————————————)   (ped: F ———————————————————)   (ped: B♭)

Exercise 30.

a) G   B♭   D   F♯ } (ped: C)   e) G♯ [C] E   (ped: D)
b) F♯   B♭   D   f) F♯ A♯ D   (ped: E)
c) F   A   C♯   (ped: G)   g) A♭ [C] E
d) G   B   D♯   (ped: A)   h) F A♭ [C] E } (ped: B♭)

Exercise 31.

a) F   A♭   C♭(B) E♭   (ped: D♭)
b) G   B♭   D♭   F   (ped: E♭)
c) G♯   B   D   F♯   (ped: E)

      ⌣ D♭9 ⌣
d) F   A♭   C♭(B) E♭   (Right Hand: G)
    (ped: D♭)
      ⌣ E♭9 ⌣
e) G   B♭   D♭   F   (Right Hand: A)
    (ped: E♭)
      ⌣ E9 ⌣
f) G♯   B   D   F♯   (Right Hand: A♯)
    (ped: E)

g) E   G   B♭   D   –F   A♭   C♭(B) E♭   –F♯   A   [C]   E   –
    (ped: C)   (ped: D♭)   (ped: D)

    G   B♭   D♭   F   –G♯   B   D   F♯
    (ped: E♭)   (ped: E)

      ⌣ C9 ⌣   ⌣ D♭9 ⌣
h) E   G   B♭   D   –   F   A♭   C♭(B) E♭   –
    (Right Hand: F♯)   (Right Hand: G)
    (ped: C)   (ped: D♭)

      ⌣ D9 ⌣   ⌣ E♭9 ⌣   ⌣ E9 ⌣
    F♯   A   [C]   E   –   G   B♭   D♭   F   –   G♯   B   D   F♯
    (Right Hand: G♯)   (Right Hand: A)   (Right Hand: A♯)
    (ped: D)   (ped: E♭)   (ped: E)

Exercise 32.

a) G   C♯   F♯   (ped: A)
b) G♭   [C]   F   (ped: A♭)
c) A♭   D   G   (ped: B♭)
        ⌣ D7 ⌣
d) F♯   A   [C]   D   (Right Hand: B)
    (ped: D)
        ⌣ F7 ⌣
e) F   A   [C]   E♭   (Right Hand: D)
    (ped: F)
        ⌣ E7 ⌣
f) G♯   B   D   E   (Right Hand: C♯)
    (ped: E)

Exercise 33.

a) G B♭ D F — B♭ E A — F A [C] E — F♯ A [C] E♭
   (ped: G)   (ped: C)   (ped: F)   (ped: F♯)

b) G C♯ F♯ — G C♯ E — G C♯ E♭ — G C♯ E
   (ped: A ———————————————————————————————)

c) A♭ D G — G C♯ F♯ — G♭ [C] F — F B E
   (ped: B♭)   (ped: A)   (ped: A♭)   (ped: G)

       ⌢ E7 ⌣   ⌢ D7 ⌣
d) G♯ B D E — G C♯ F♯ — F♯ A [C] E — F♯ A [C] D — G B D E
   (ped: E)   (ped: A)   (ped: D ———————————————)   (ped: G)

          ⌢ Cm7 ⌣   ⌢ F7 ⌣
e) G B♭ D E — G B♭ [C] E♭ — F A [C] E♭ — F A B♭ D
   (ped: C ———————————————————————————)   (ped: F)   (ped: B♭)

Exercise 34.

         a) G C♯ F   (ped: A)   ⌢ D7 ⌣
         b) G♭ [C] F♭   (ped: A♭)   f) F♯ A [C] D
         c) A♭ D G♭   (ped: B♭)   (R.H.: B♭) (ped: D)
                                              ⌢ F7 ⌣
         d) A D♯ G   (ped: B)   g) F A [C] E♭
         e) A D♯ G♯   (ped: B)   (R.H.: D♭) (ped: F)
                                              ⌢ E7 ⌣
                                         h) G♯ B D E
                                             (R.H.: C) (ped: E)

Exercise 35.

a) F B E — F B E♭ — F A [C] D — F G B D♯ — G B [C] E
   (ped: G ———————————)   (ped: D)   (ped: G)   (ped: C)

b) A♭ D G — A♭ D G♭ — G C♯ F♯ — G C♯ F — F A B E
   (ped: B♭ ———————————)   (ped: A ———————————)   (ped: D)

c) G C♯ E♭ — G C♯ E — G C♯ E♯ — G C♯ F♯ — G C♯ F — G C♯ E
   (ped: A ——)

       ⌢ E7 ⌣   ⌢ F7 ⌣   ⌢ E7 ⌣
d) G♯ B D E — (Same) — F A [C] E♭ — (Same) — G♯ B D E — (Same)
   (ped: E ———————————)   (ped: F ———————————)   (ped: E ———————————)

102

~ C7 ~   ~ B7 ~   ~ E7 ~

e)   G   Bb   [C]   E   – (Same)   – F#   A   B   D#   – (Same)   – G#   B   D   E

(ped: C ——————————)   (ped: B ——————————)   (ped: E)

Exercise 36.

a)   G   B   D#   F#   – G   B   C#   E   – F#   A   [C]   E   – F   A   B   E   – G   B   D   E

(ped: A ——————————————————)   (ped: D)   (ped: G)   (ped: C)

b)   G   B   C#   F#   – G   B   C#   F   – F#   A   [C]   E   – F   Ab   B   E   – G   B   D   E

(ped: A ——————————————————)   (ped: D)   (ped: G)   (ped: C)

c)   G   B   D   F#   – G   Bb   C#   F   – G   A   [C]   E   – Gb   Bb   [C]   F   – F#   A   B   D

(ped: A ———————————————————————————)   (ped: Ab)   (ped: G)

~ C11 ~   ~ C–9 ~   ~ F–9 ~   ~ Bb ~

d)   G   Bb   D   F   – G   Bb   Db   E   – G   Bb   [C]   Eb   – Gb   A   [C]   Eb   – F   Bb   D

(ped: C ———————————————————————————————)   (ped: F)   (ped: Bb)

~ D9 ~   ~ D–9 ~   ~ G13 ~   ~ G–13 ~   ~ C9 (Low) ~

e)   F#   A   [C]   E   – F#   A   [C]   Eb   – F   B   E   – F   B   Eb   – E   G   Bb   D

(ped: D ————————————————————)   (ped: G ——————————)   (ped: C)

Exercise 37.

~ Gm7 (High) ~   ~ C7 ~   ~ C7–5 ~   ~ Fmaj7* ~

a)   G   Bb   D   F   – (Same)   – G   Bb   [C]   E   – Gb   Bb   [C]   E   – F   A   [C]   E

(ped: G ——————————)   (ped: C ———————————————————)   (ped: F)

~ G7–5 ~   ~ C–9 ~   ~ C–9–5 ~   ~ Fmaj7 ~

b)   F   G   B   Db   – (Same)   – G   Bb   Db   E   – Gb   Bb   Db   E   – F   A   [C]   E

(ped: G ——————————)   (ped: C ———————————————————)   (ped: F)

~ D+9 ~

c)   G   A   [C]   E   – F#   [C]   E#(F)

(ped: A)   (ped: D)

~ D9+5 ~

d)   G   A   [C]   E   – F#   A#   [C]   E

(ped: A)   (ped: D)

~ F7–5 ~   ~ Bb7–5 (Low) ~

e)   G   Bb   [C]   Eb   – F   A   Cb(B)   Eb   – Fb(E)   Ab   Bb   D

(ped: C)   (ped: F)   (ped: Bb)

* 4 note chord more convenient here. The fact that the "maj7" (E) is also in the Right Hand does not matter.

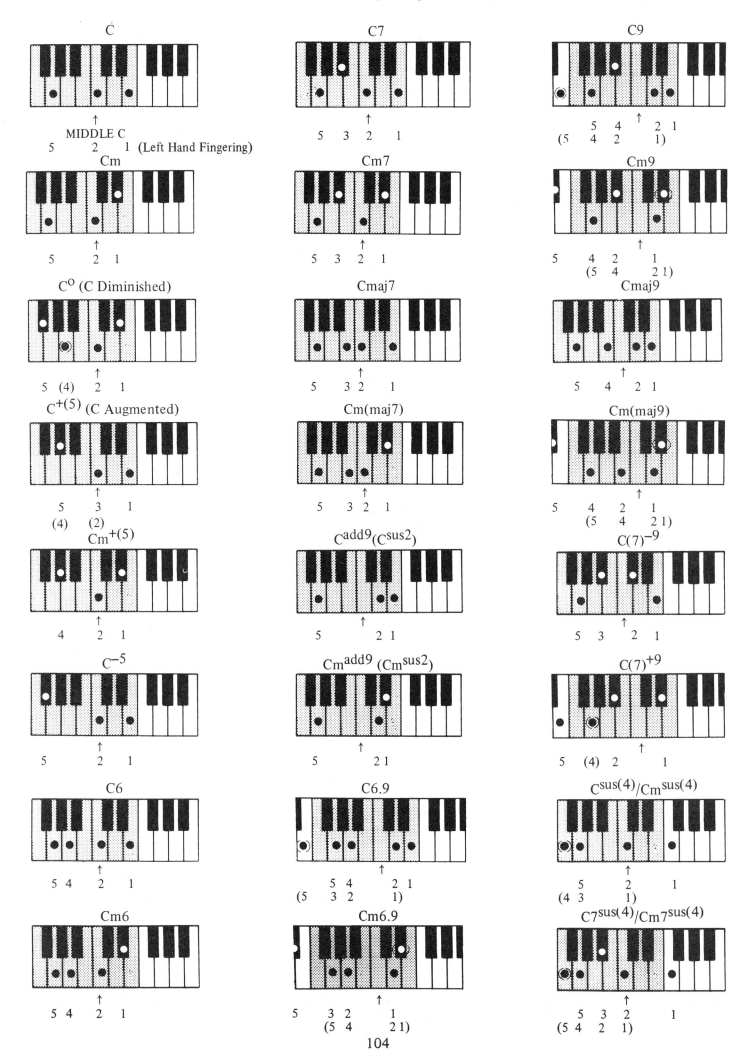

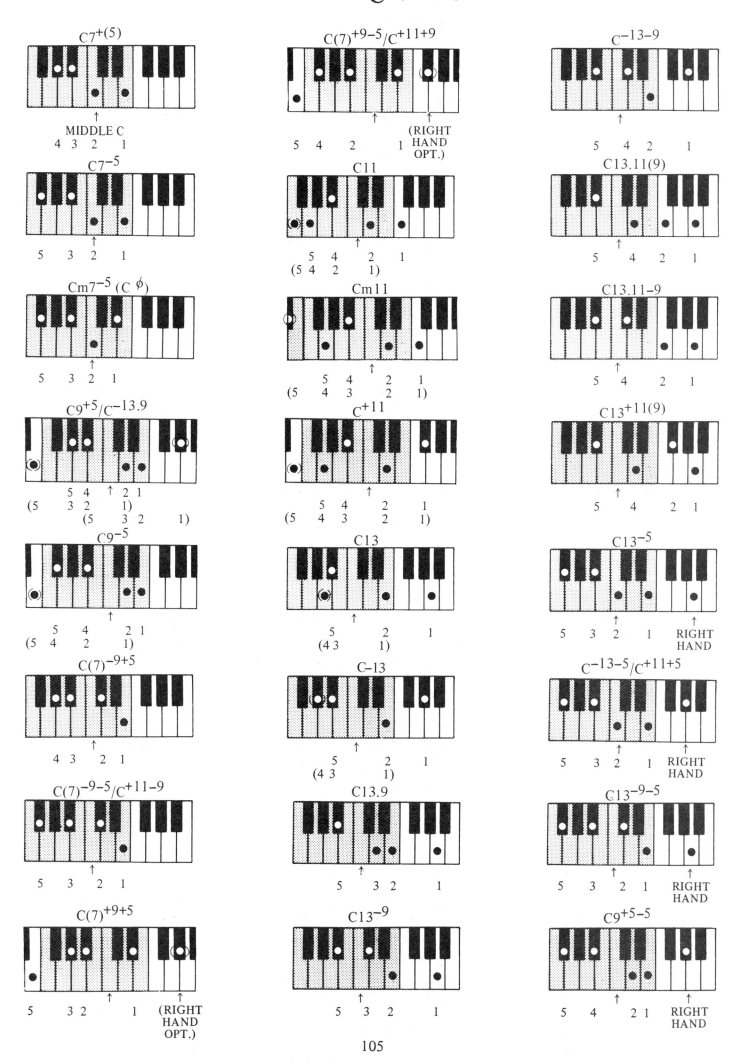

Db (C#) (Organ Pedal: Db (C#))

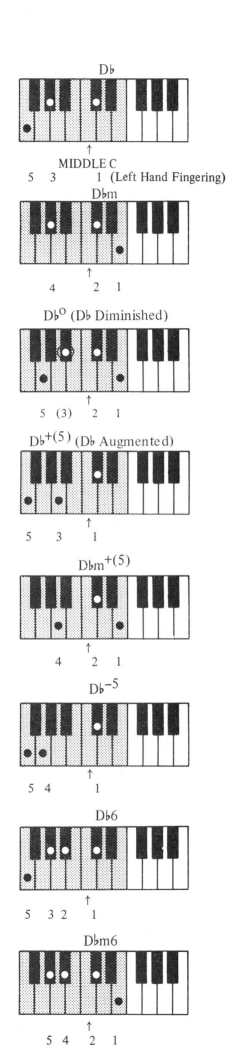

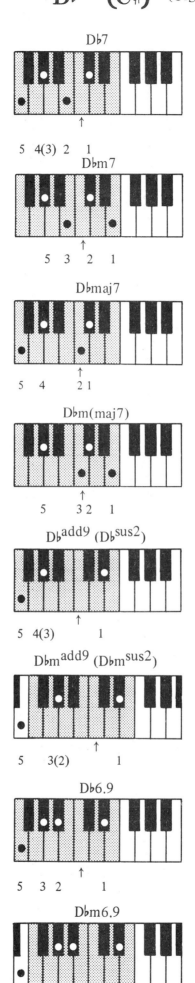

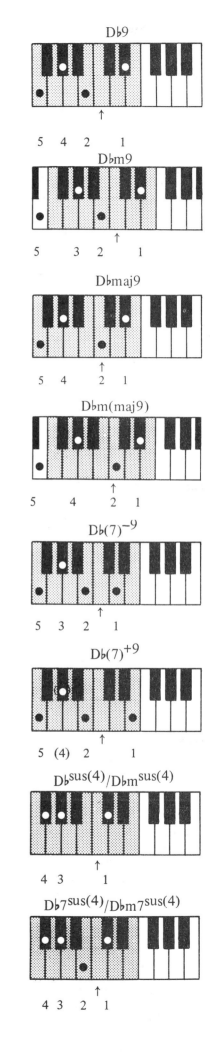

106

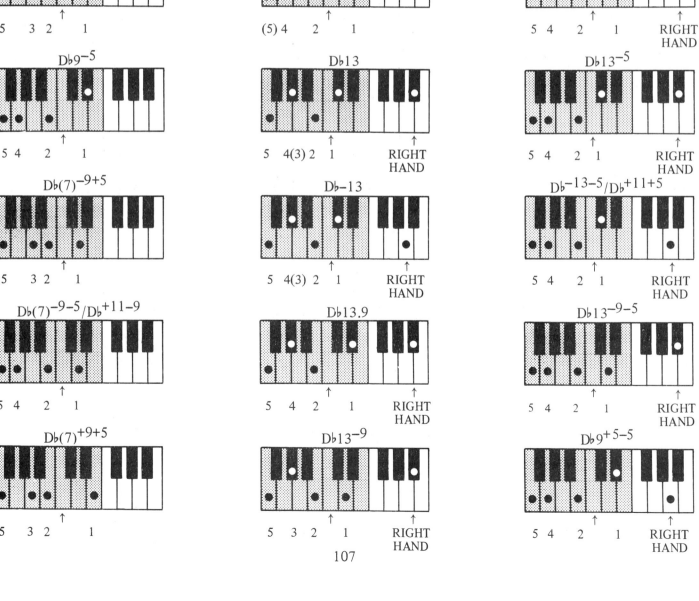

D♭7+(5)

MIDDLE C
5   3 2   1

D♭(7)+9−5/D♭+11+9
5 4   2   1

D♭−13−9
5   3 2   1   RIGHT HAND

D♭7−5
5 4   2 1

D♭11
5 4· 2   1

D♭13.11(9)
5 4   2   1   RIGHT HAND

D♭m7−5 (D♭ø)
5   3 2   1

D♭m11
(5   5   4   2   1
    4   3   2   1)

D♭13.11−9
5 4   2   1   RIGHT HAND

D♭9+5/D♭−13.9
5   3 2   1

D♭+11
(5) 4   2   1

D♭13+11(9)
5 4   2   1   RIGHT HAND

D♭9−5
5 4   2   1

D♭13
5 4(3) 2 1   RIGHT HAND

D♭13−5
5 4   2 1   RIGHT HAND

D♭(7)−9+5
5   3 2   1

D♭−13
5 4(3) 2 1   RIGHT HAND

D♭−13−5/D♭+11+5
5 4   2 1   RIGHT HAND

D♭(7)−9−5/D♭+11−9
5 4   2   1

D♭13.9
5 4   2   1   RIGHT HAND

D♭13−9−5
5 4   2   1   RIGHT HAND

D♭(7)+9+5
5   3 2   1

D♭13−9
5   3 2   1   RIGHT HAND

D♭9+5−5
5 4   2   1   RIGHT HAND

D (Organic Pedal: D)

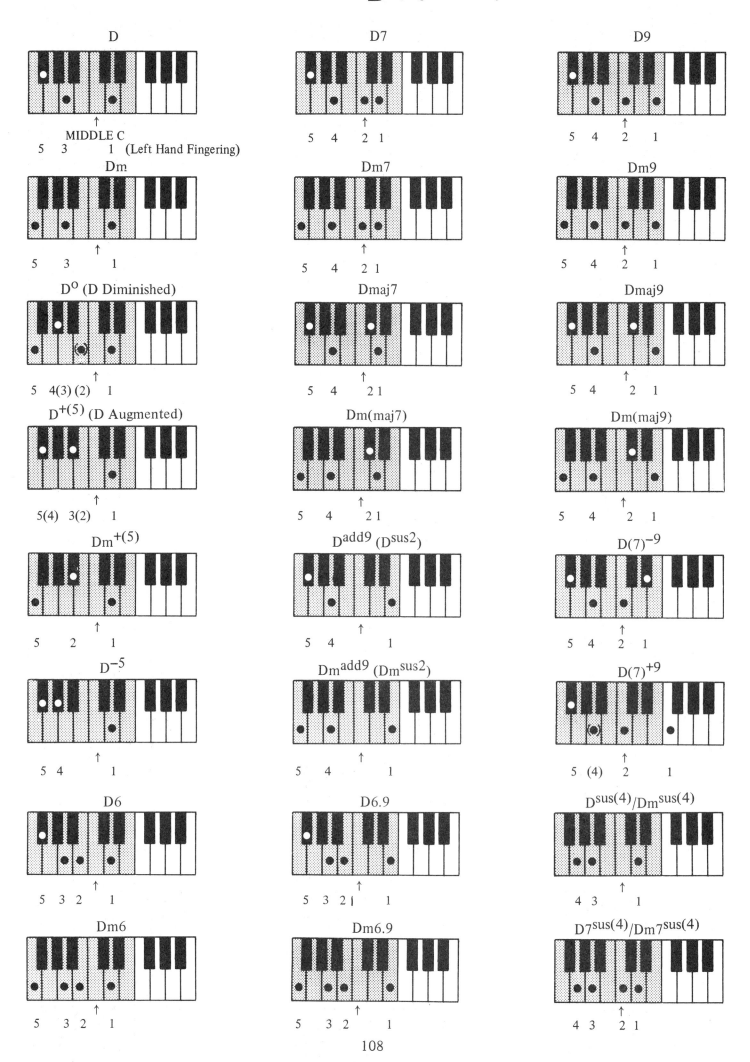

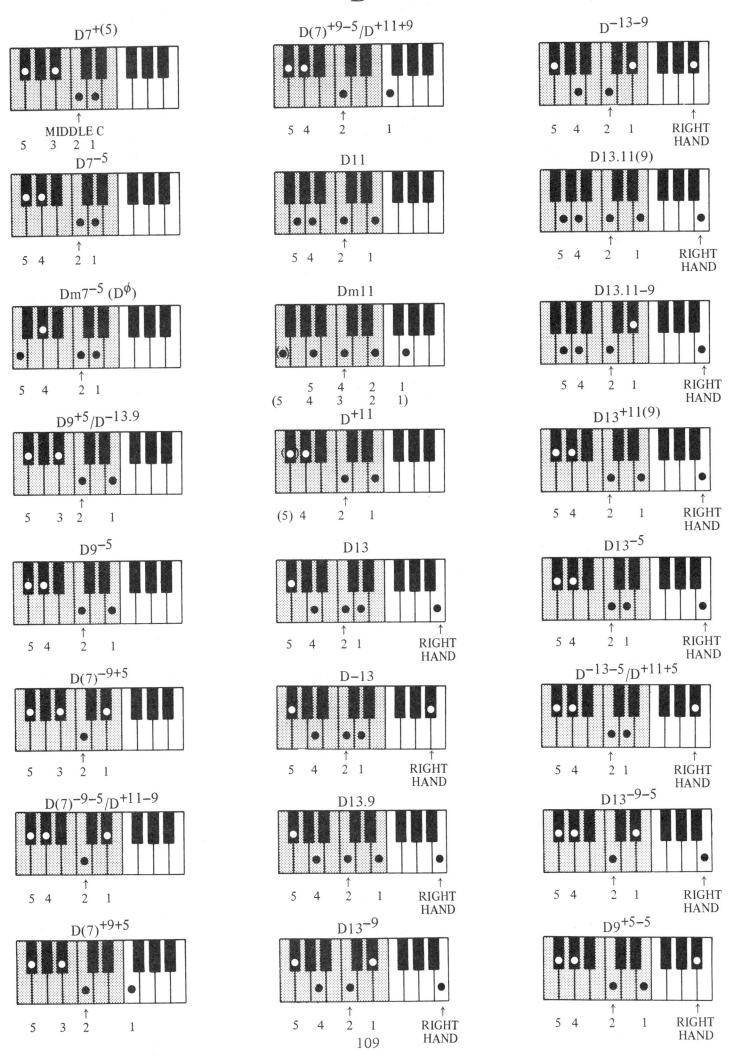

D (Pedal : D)

109

E♭ (D#) (Organ Pedal: E♭ (D#))

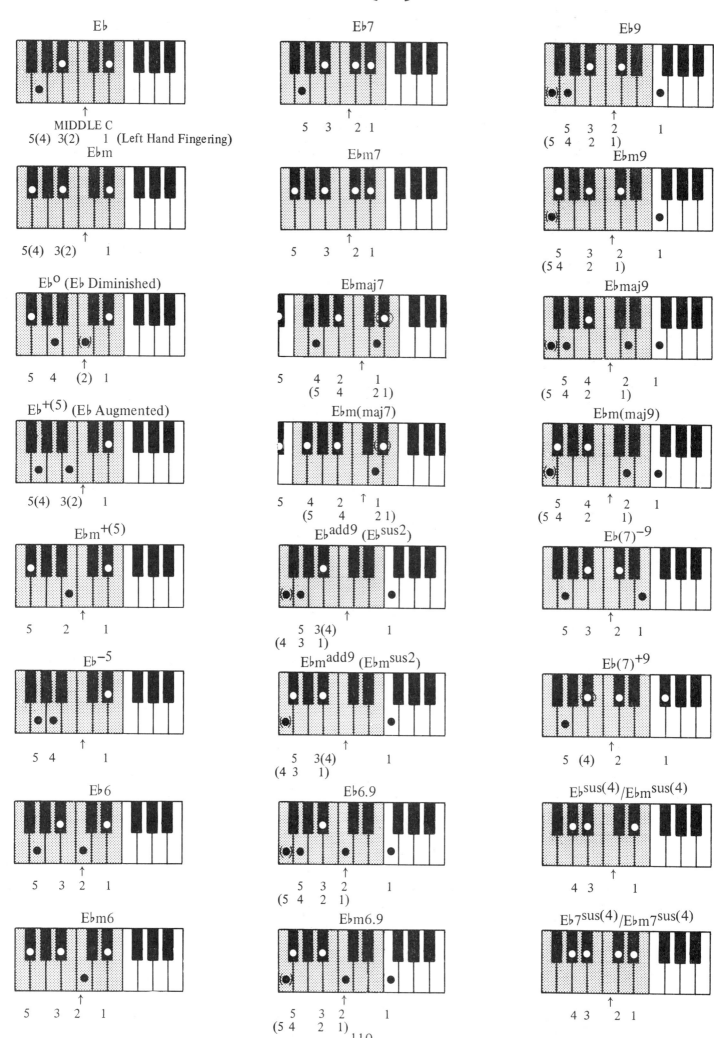

110

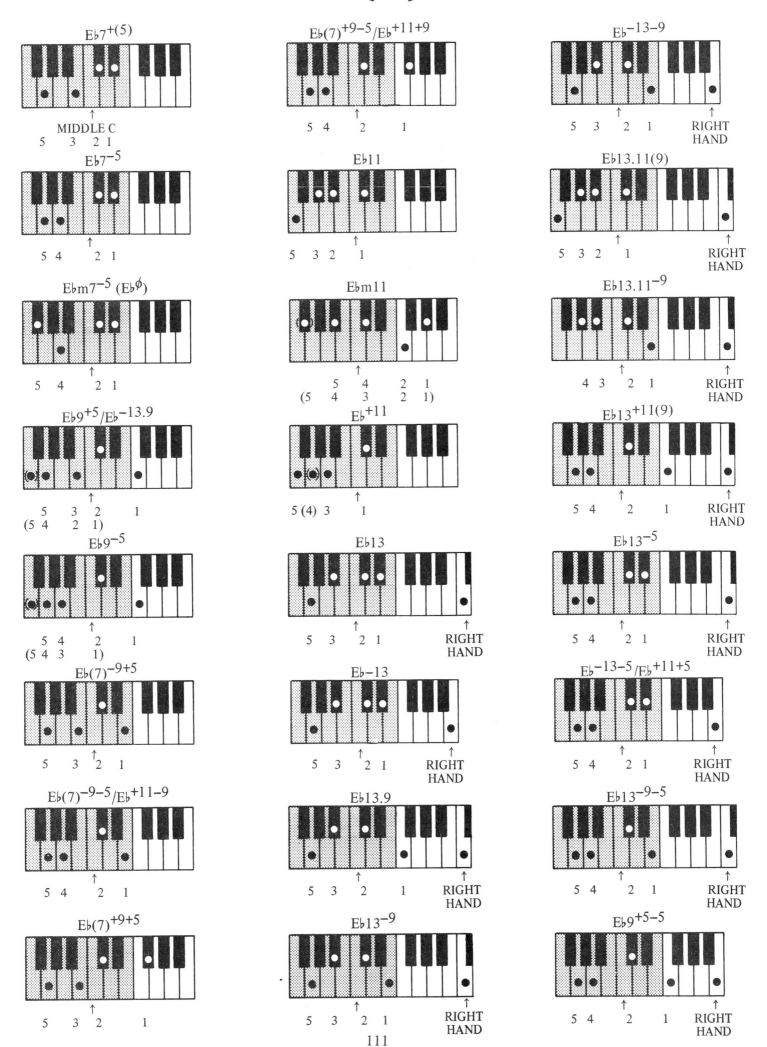

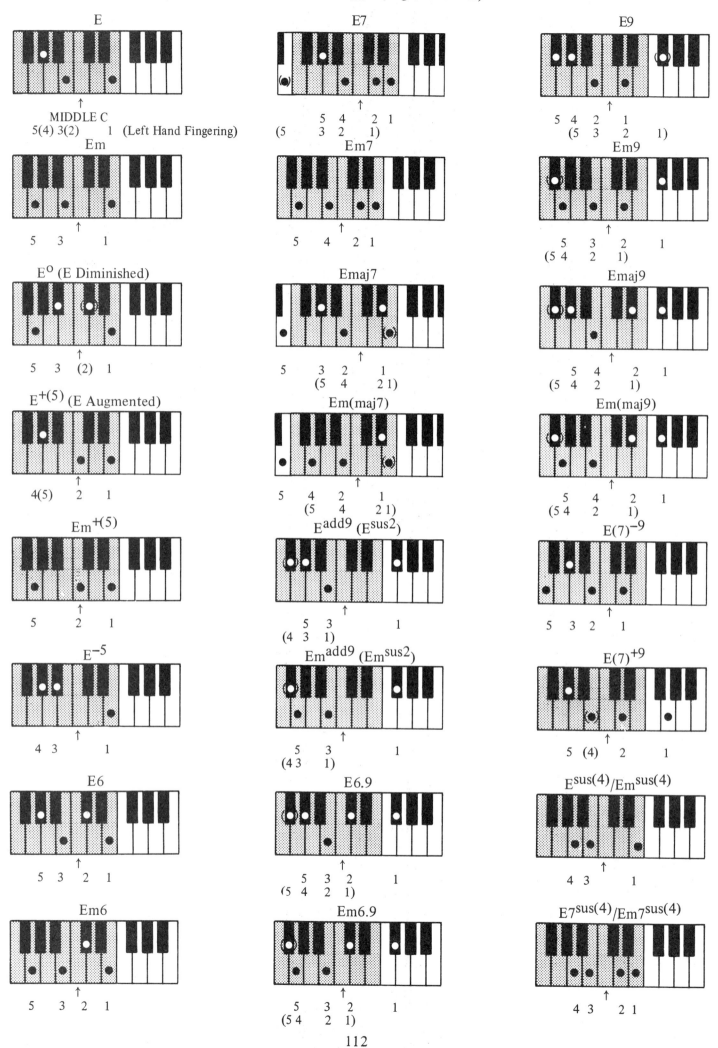

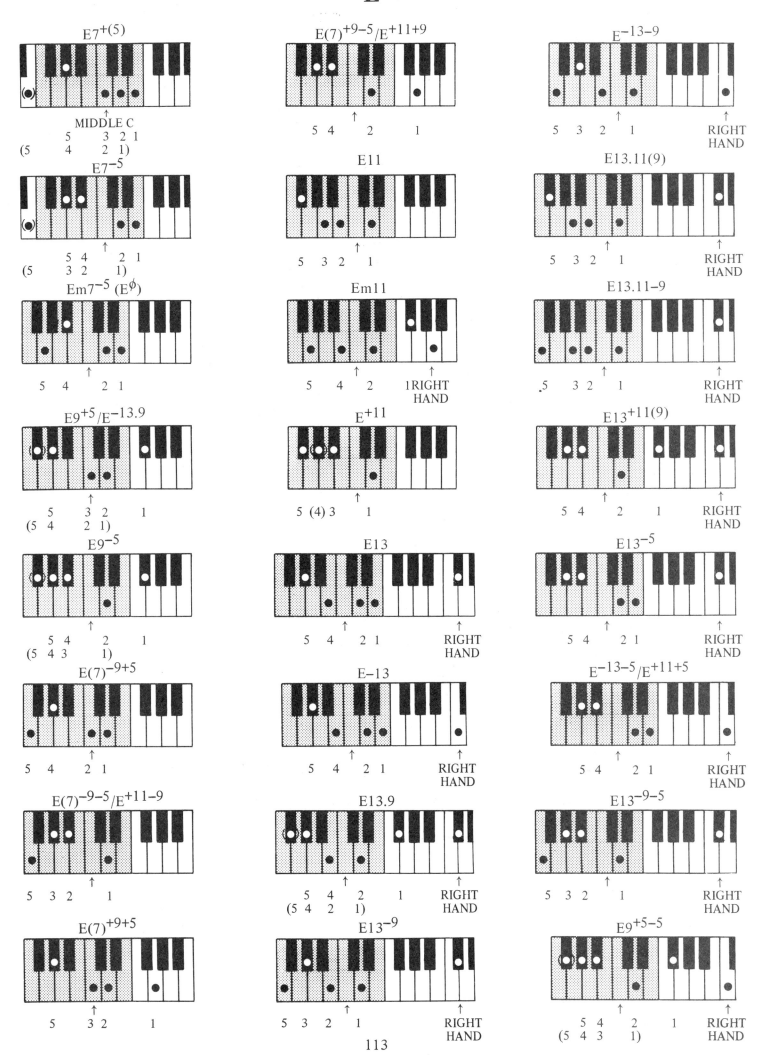

E (Pedal: E)

113

F (Organ Pedal: F)

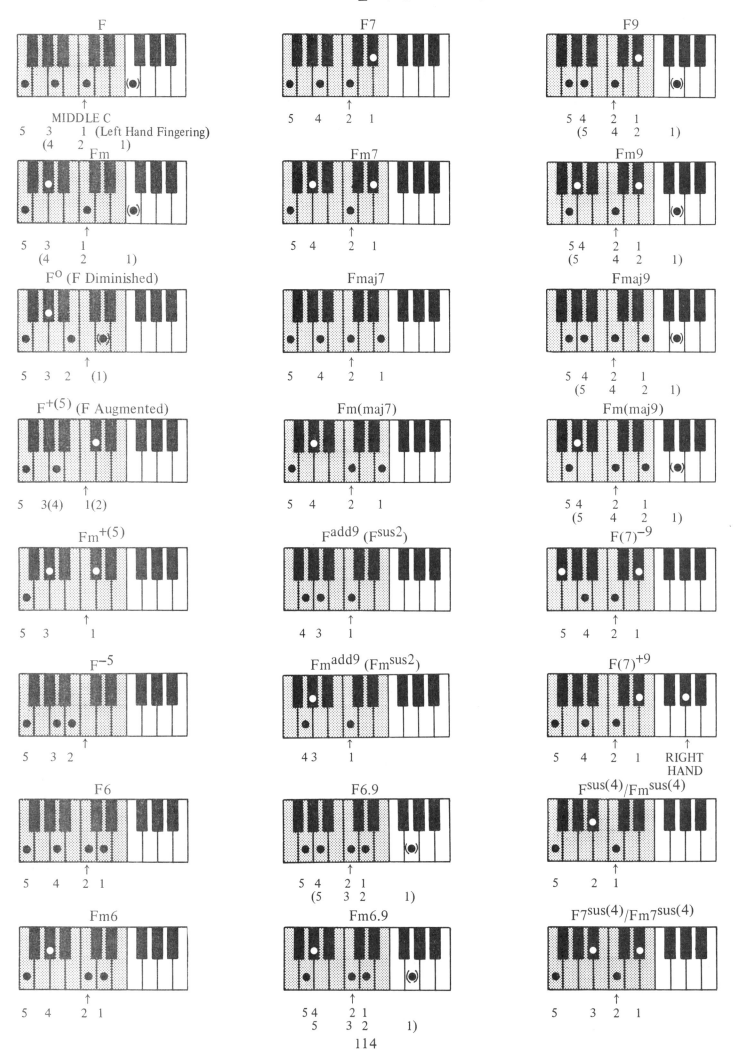

F (Pedal: F)

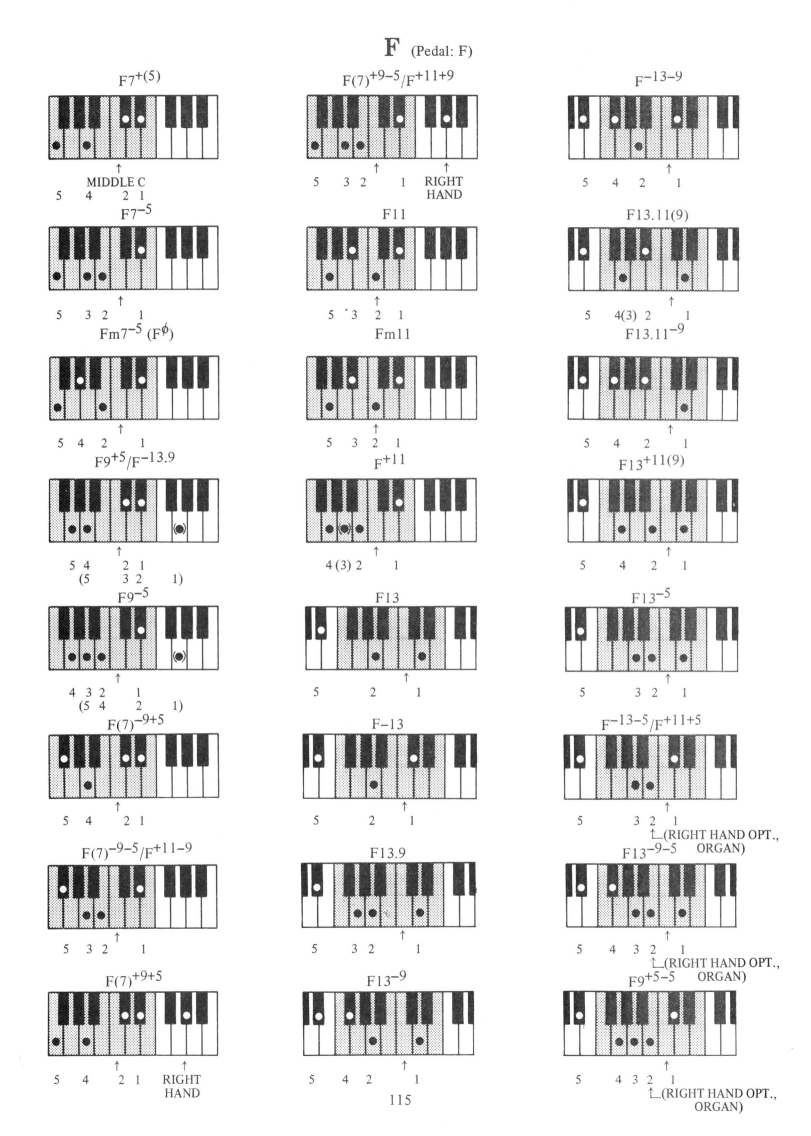

G♭ (F♯) (Organ Pedal: G♭ (F♯))

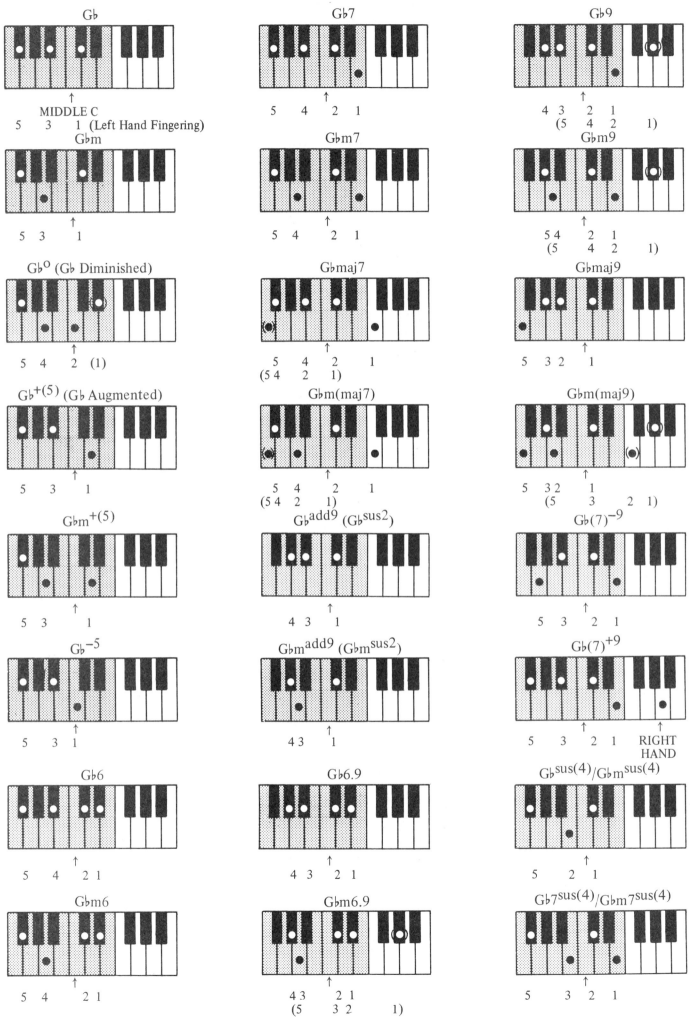

116

Gb (F#) (Pedal: Gb(F#))

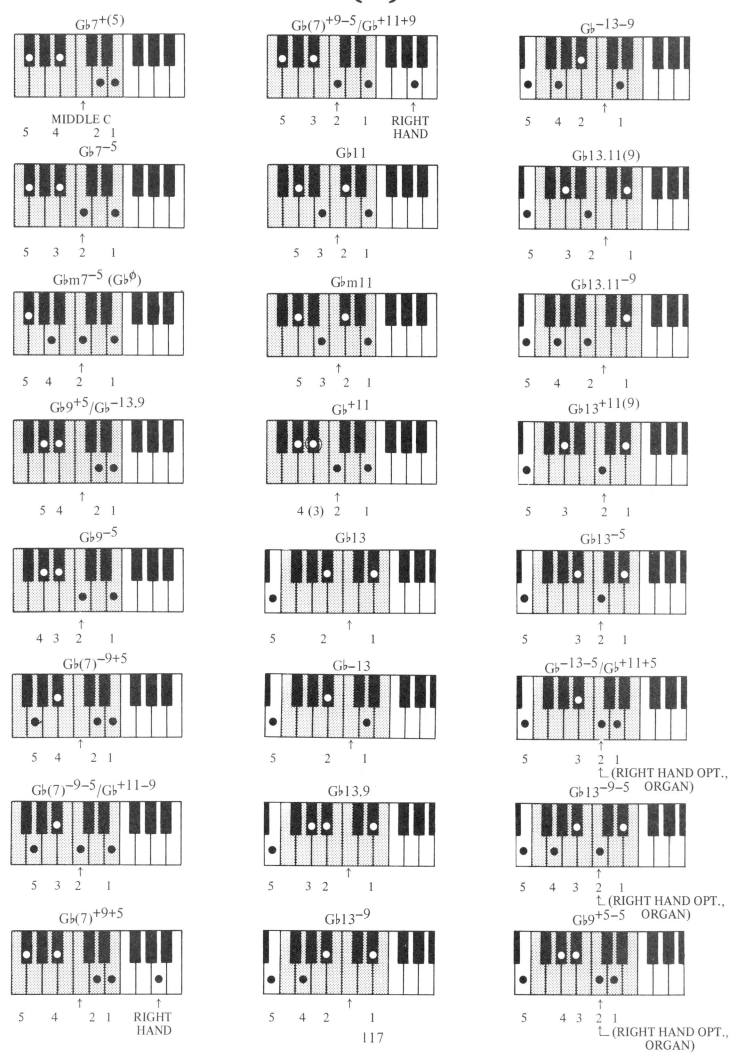

Gb7+(5)

MIDDLE C

5 4 2 1

Gb(7)+9-5/Gb+11+9

5 3 2 1 RIGHT HAND

Gb-13-9

5 4 2 1

Gb7-5

5 3 2 1

Gb11

5 3 2 1

Gb13.11(9)

5 3 2 1

Gbm7-5 (Gbø)

5 4 2 1

Gbm11

5 3 2 1

Gb13.11-9

5 4 2 1

Gb9+5/Gb-13.9

5 4 2 1

Gb+11

4 (3) 2 1

Gb13+11(9)

5 3 2 1

Gb9-5

4 3 2 1

Gb13

5 2 1

Gb13-5

5 3 2 1

Gb(7)-9+5

5 4 2 1

Gb-13

5 2 1

Gb-13-5/Gb+11+5

5 3 2 1
↰ (RIGHT HAND OPT., ORGAN)

Gb(7)-9-5/Gb+11-9

5 3 2 1

Gb13.9

5 3 2 1

Gb13-9-5

5 4 3 2 1
↰ (RIGHT HAND OPT., ORGAN)

Gb(7)+9+5

5 4 2 1 RIGHT HAND

Gb13-9

5 4 2 1

Gb9+5-5

5 4 3 2 1
↰ (RIGHT HAND OPT., ORGAN)

117

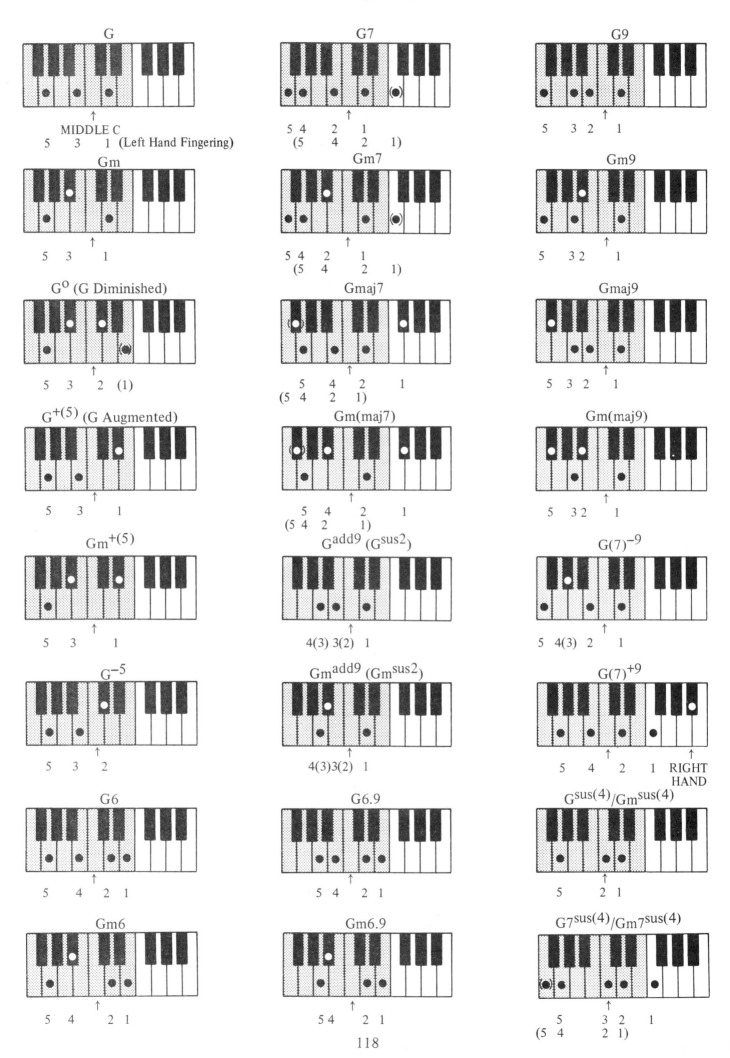

G

MIDDLE C

5   3   1   (Left Hand Fingering)

Gm

5   3   1

Gᵒ (G Diminished)

5   3   2   (1)

G⁺⁽⁵⁾ (G Augmented)

5   3   1

Gm⁺⁽⁵⁾

5   3   1

G⁻⁵

5   3   2

G6

5   4   2   1

Gm6

5   4   2   1

G7

5   4   2   1
(5   4   2   1)

Gm7

5   4   2   1
(5   4   2   1)

Gmaj7

5   4   2   1
(5   4   2   1)

Gm(maj7)

5   4   2   1
(5   4   2   1)

Gᵃᵈᵈ⁹ (Gˢᵘˢ²)

4(3)   3(2)   1

Gmᵃᵈᵈ⁹ (Gmˢᵘˢ²)

4(3)   3(2)   1

G6.9

5   4   2   1

Gm6.9

5   4   2   1

G9

5   3   2   1

Gm9

5   3   2   1

Gmaj9

5   3   2   1

Gm(maj9)

5   3   2   1

G(7)⁻⁹

5   4(3)   2   1

G(7)⁺⁹

5   4   2   1   RIGHT HAND

Gˢᵘˢ⁽⁴⁾/Gmˢᵘˢ⁽⁴⁾

5   2   1

G7ˢᵘˢ⁽⁴⁾/Gm7ˢᵘˢ⁽⁴⁾

5   3   2   1
(5   4   2   1)

118

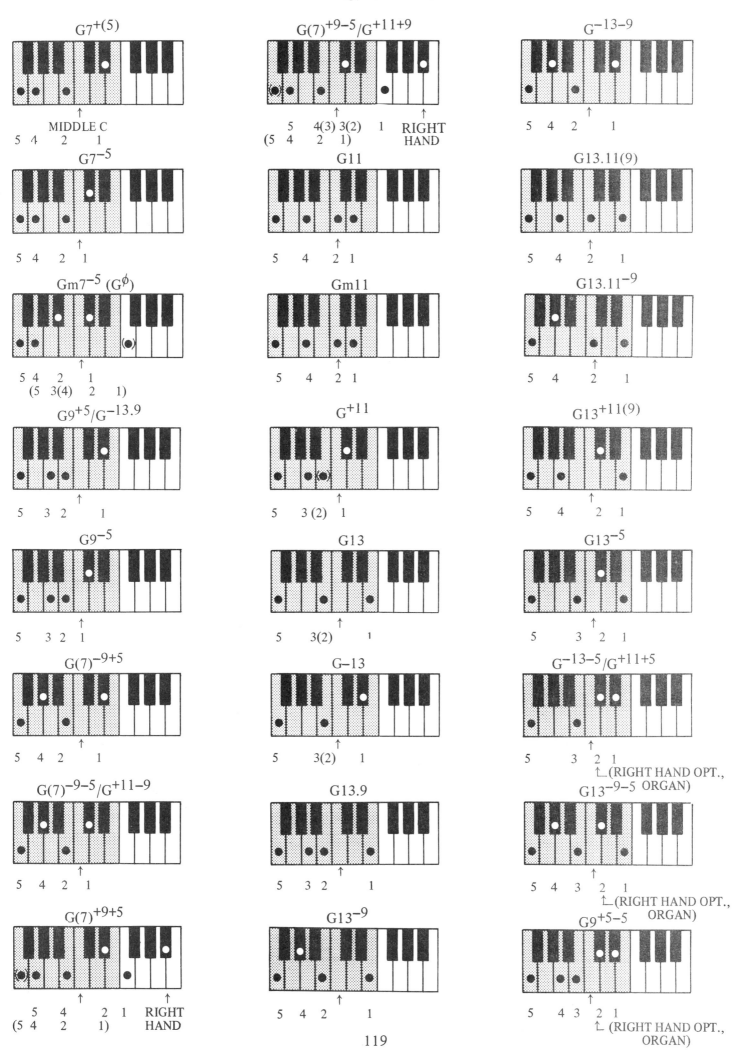

G (Pedal : G)

119

A♭ (G♯) (Pedal: A♭(G♯))

A♭7$^{+(5)}$

MIDDLE C
5 4   2 1

A♭7^{-5}

5 4   2 1

A♭m7^{-5} (A♭∅)

5 4 2   1

A♭9^{+5}/A♭$^{-13.9}$

5 3 2 1

A♭9^{-5}

5 3 2 1

A♭(7)$^{-9+5}$

5 4 2 1

A♭(7)$^{-9-5}$/A♭$^{+11-9}$

5 4 2 1

A♭(7)$^{+9+5}$

5 4   2   RIGHT HAND

A♭(7)$^{+9-5}$/A♭$^{+11+9}$

5 4   2 1   RIGHT HAND

A♭11

5   4(3) 2 1

A♭m11

5   4(3) 2 1

A♭$^{+11}$

5 3 (2) 1

A♭13

5   2   1

A♭-13

5   2   1

A♭13.9

5 3 2   1

A♭13^{-9}

5 4   2   1

121

A♭$^{-13-9}$

5 4   2 1

A♭13.11(9)

5 3   2   1

A♭13.11^{-9}

5 4   2   1

A♭13$^{+11(9)}$

5 4   2   1

A♭13^{-5}

5 3 2   1

A♭$^{-13-5}$/A♭$^{+11+5}$

5   3 2 1

⌐ (RIGHT HAND OPT., ORGAN)

A♭13^{-9-5}

5 4 3 2   1

⌐ (RIGHT HAND OPT., ORGAN)

A♭9^{+5-5}

5 4 3 2 1

⌐ (RIGHT HAND OPT., ORGAN)

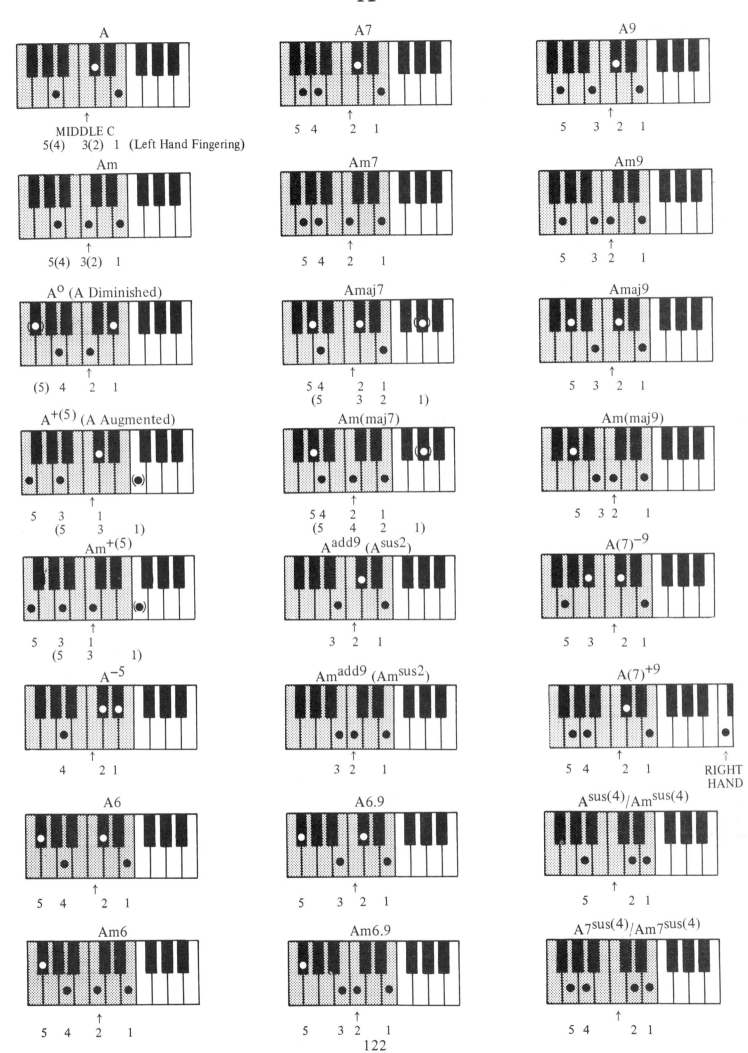

A (Organ Pedal: A)

122

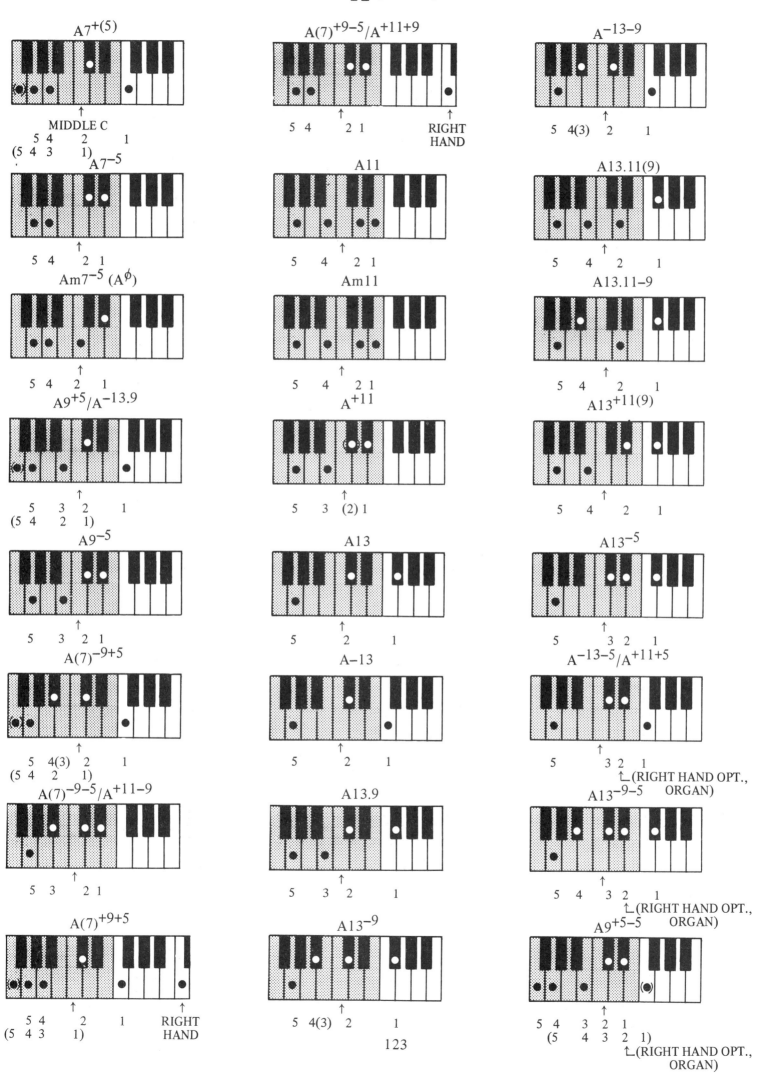

A7⁺⁽⁵⁾

MIDDLE C

5 4   2   1
(5 4 3   1)

A(7)⁺⁹⁻⁵/A⁺¹¹⁺⁹

5 4   2 1   RIGHT
                               HAND

A⁻¹³⁻⁹

5 4(3)   2   1

A7⁻⁵

5 4   2 1

A11

5 4   2 1

A13.11(9)

5 4   2   1

Am7⁻⁵ (Aᵠ)

5 4   2 1

Am11

5 4   2 1

A13.11⁻⁹

5 4   2   1

A9⁺⁵/A⁻¹³·⁹

5   3   2   1
(5 4   2 1)

A⁺¹¹

5   3 (2) 1

A13⁺¹¹⁽⁹⁾

5 4   2   1

A9⁻⁵

5   3 2 1

A13

5   2   1

A13⁻⁵

5   3 2 1

A(7)⁻⁹⁺⁵

5 4(3) 2   1
(5 4 2 1)

A⁻¹³

5   2   1

A⁻¹³⁻⁵/A⁺¹¹⁺⁵

5   3 2 1

⌐(RIGHT HAND OPT.,
    ORGAN)

A(7)⁻⁹⁻⁵/A⁺¹¹⁻⁹

5 3   2 1

A13.9

5 3 2   1

A13⁻⁹⁻⁵

5 4   3 2   1

⌐(RIGHT HAND OPT.,
    ORGAN)

A(7)⁺⁹⁺⁵

5 4   2   1   RIGHT
(5 4 3   1)   HAND

A13⁻⁹

5 4(3) 2   1

123

A9⁺⁵⁻⁵

5 4   3 2 1   (·)
(5   4 3 2 1)

⌐(RIGHT HAND OPT.,
    ORGAN)

B♭ (A♯) (Organ Pedal: B♭ (A♯))

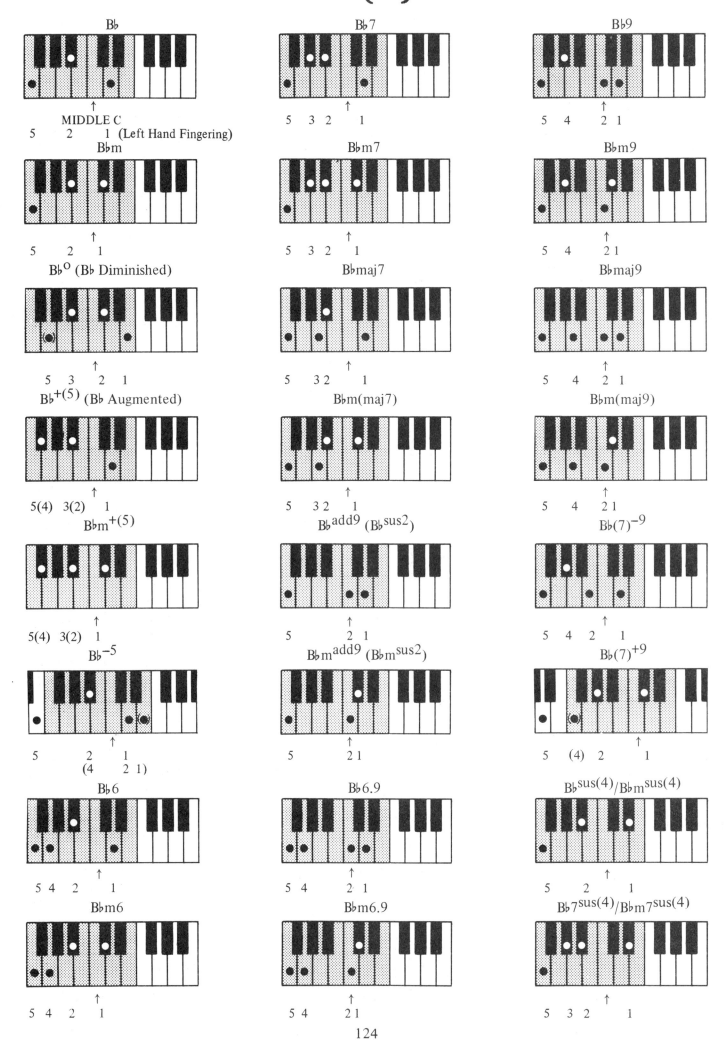

B♭ (A♯) (Pedal: B♭(A♯))

B♭7+(5)

MIDDLE C
4 3 2   1

B♭7−5

(5
      5 4   2 1
      3 2   1)

B♭m7−5 (B♭ø)

5 4   2 1

B♭9+5/B♭−13.9

5 4   2 1

B♭9−5

(5
      5   3 2 1
      3   2 1)

B♭(7)−9+5

5 4 2   1

B♭(7)−9−5/B♭+11−9

(5
      5 4   2 1
      3 2   1)

B♭(7)+9+5

5   3 2   1

B♭(7)+9−5/B♭+11+9

5 4   2   1

B♭11

5 4   2 1

B♭m11

5 4   2 1

B♭+11

5   3 (2) 1

B♭13

5   2   1

B♭−13

5   2   1

B♭13.9

5   3 2   1

B♭13−9

5 4(3)   2   1

125

B♭−13−9

5 4(3) 2   1

B♭13.11(9)

5   3 2   1

B♭13.11−9

5 4   2   1

B♭13+11(9)

5   4   2   1

B♭13−5

5   3 2   1

B♭−13−5/B♭+11+5

5   3 2 1
⌐(RIGHT HAND OPT.,
   ORGAN)

B♭13−9−5

5 4   3 2   1
⌐(RIGHT HAND OPT.,
   ORGAN)

B♭9+5−5

5   4   3 2   1
(RIGHT HAND OPT.,
   ORGAN)

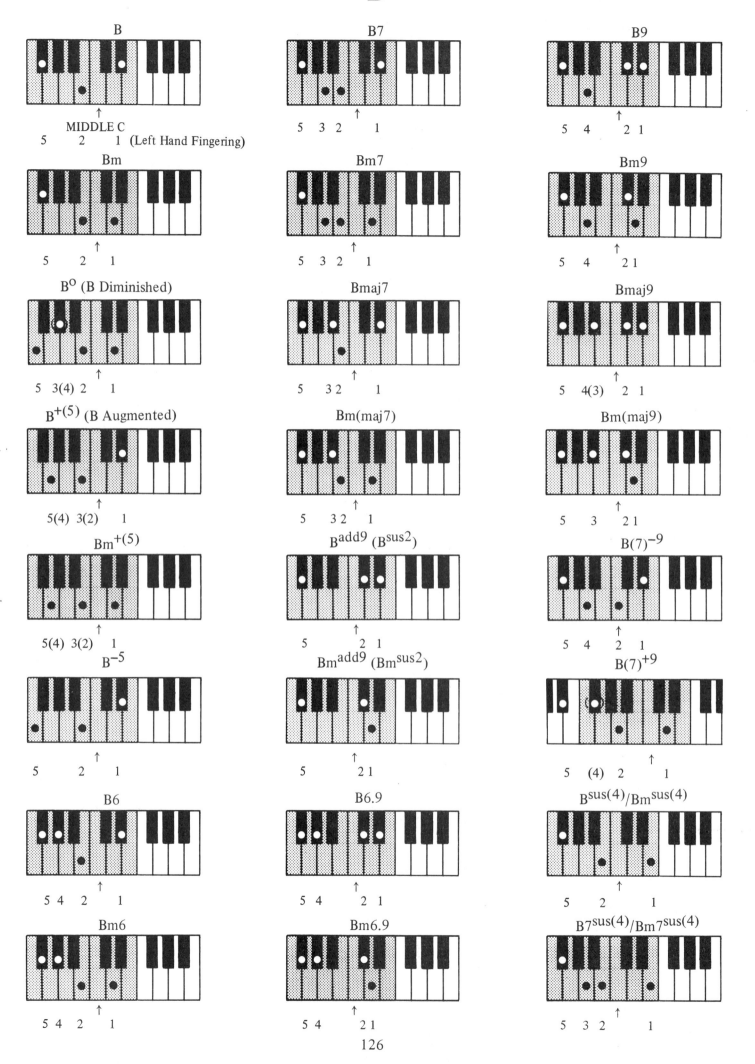

B (Organ Pedal: B)

B

MIDDLE C
5   2   1 (Left Hand Fingering)

Bm

5   2   1

B° (B Diminished)

5 3(4) 2   1

B⁺⁽⁵⁾ (B Augmented)

5(4) 3(2)   1

Bm⁺⁽⁵⁾

5(4) 3(2)   1

B⁻⁵

5   2   1

B6

5 4 2   1

Bm6

5 4 2   1

B7

5 3 2   1

Bm7

5 3 2   1

Bmaj7

5 3 2   1

Bm(maj7)

5   3 2 1

B^add9 (B^sus2)

5   2 1

Bm^add9 (Bm^sus2)

5   2 1

B6.9

5 4   2 1

Bm6.9

5 4   2 1

B9

5 4   2 1

Bm9

5 4   2 1

Bmaj9

5 4(3) 2 1

Bm(maj9)

5   3   2 1

B(7)⁻⁹

5 4 2 1

B(7)⁺⁹

5 (4) 2   1

B^sus(4)/Bm^sus(4)

5   2   1

B7^sus(4)/Bm7^sus(4)

5 3 2   1

126

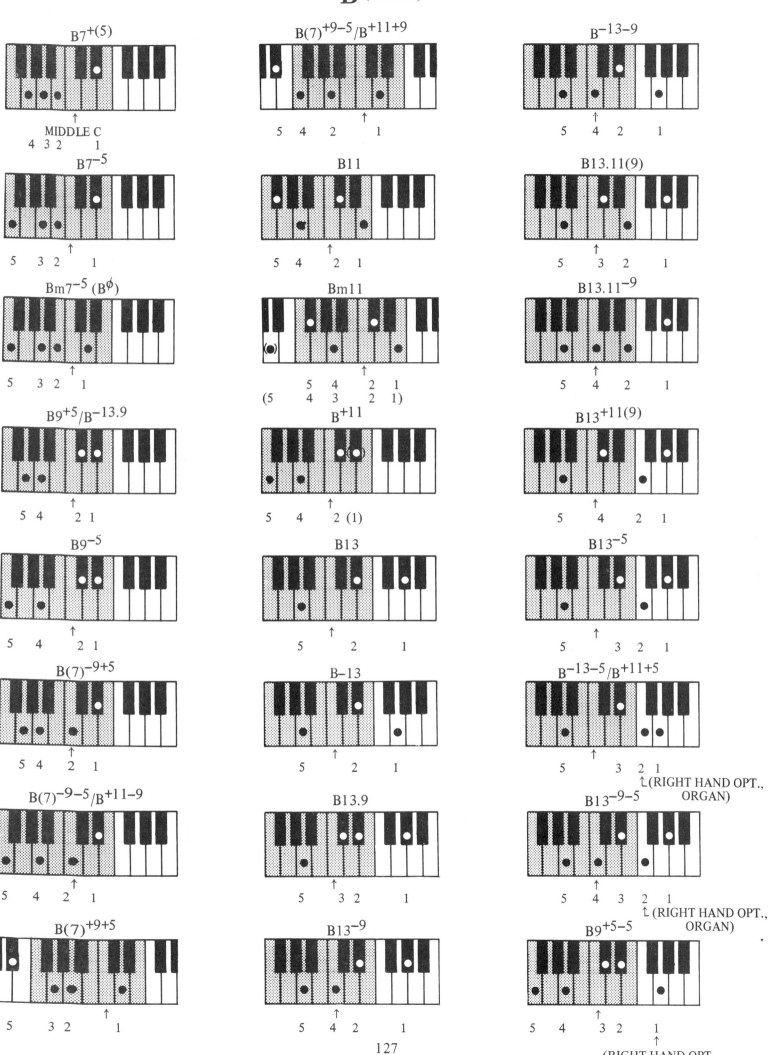

ALTERNATIVE CHORD SYMBOLS

Since chord symbols are constantly evolving it would be impossible to list all existing variations world-wide.

The following information may, however, be of some help:

In general:—

$$+ \quad = \sharp$$
$$- \quad = \flat$$

Chord Name	Alternative Chord Symbols
C Diminished (7th)	C^o, C^o7, Cdim, Cdim7
C Augmented (5th)	C+, C+5, C$\sharp$5, Caug
C Minor with Augmented 5th	Cm+5, Cm+
C Major 7th	Cmaj7, Cma7, CM7, C$\sharp$7, C$\triangle$7
C Minor with Major 7th	Cm(maj7), Cm($\sharp$7), Cm(M7)
C Major with Added 9th (C Major suspended 2nd)	Cadd9, Csus 2
C Minor with Added 9th (C Minor suspended 2nd)	Cm^{add9}, Cm^{sus2}
C Dominant 7th with Augmented 5th	C7+, C7+5, C7$\sharp$5, C+7, C7aug
C Dominant 7th with flattened (flatted, or flat) 9th	C−9, C$\flat$9, C7−9, C7$\flat$9
C Dominant 7th with sharpened (sharped, sharp, or augmented) 9th	C+9, C$\sharp$9, C7+9, C7$\sharp$9
C Suspended 4th	Csus4, Csus
C Minor suspended 4th	Cm^{sus4}, Cm^{sus}
C Dominant 7th suspended 4th	C7sus4, C7sus
C Minor 7th suspended 4th	Cm7sus4, Cm7sus
C Minor 7th with Diminished (flattened, flatted, or flat) 5th (C Half-diminished 7th)	Cm7−5, Cm7$\flat$5, C$^\emptyset$
C Dominant 9th with augmented 5th	C9+5, C9+, C9$\sharp$5, C9aug